ENGAGEMENT WITH GOD

HANS URS VON BALTHASAR

ENGAGEMENT WITH GOD

The Drama of Christian Discipleship

Translated by
R. JOHN HALLIBURTON

Foreword by
DR. MARGARET TUREK

IGNATIUS PRESS   SAN FRANCISCO

Original German edition:
In Gottes Einsatz leben
© 1971, 2nd ed. 1972, by
Johannes Verlag, Einsiedeln

English translation © 1975 by
The Society for Promoting Christian Knowledge, London
All rights reserved
© 1986, 2nd Edition, Editoriale Jaca Book S.p.A., Milan
English language edition published by arrangement with
Literary Agency Eulama Srl, Rome

Cover art:
Crucifixion (detail)
Cimabue (1240–1302)
San Domenico, Arezzo, Italy
© Scala/Art Resource, New York

Cover design by Roxanne Mei Lum

This edition published in 2008 by
Ignatius Press, San Francisco
Forward copyright 2008 by Ignatius Press
All rights reserved
ISBN 978-1-58617-196-4
Library of Congress Control Number 2007933596
Printed in the United States of America ∞

CONTENTS

Foreword, by Dr. Margaret M. Turek   vii
Translator's Note   xiii
Preface   1

PART ONE: THE DIVINE INVOLVEMENT

1. The Meaning of the Old Testament   13
    God's involvement in choosing   13
    The chosen   18
    The encounter between the chooser and the chosen   20

2. The Meaning of the New Covenant   25
    Jesus as God's involvement   25
    The chosen   29
    The encounter between the chooser and the chosen   35

3. Some Conclusions   42
    Tidings of joy: abiding in the source   42
    Considering our neighbor   51
    The Christian hope   56

PART TWO: OUR INVOLVEMENT

4. Introductory   65
    Man in relation to God   65
    A negative proof   71
    The example of the God-Man   77

5. The Christian and the World 82
   Things and their value 82
   The opposition of structures 85
   Work and witness 90

6. The Joy of the Cross 94
   "Falling into the earth" 94
   A sign of joy in the universal darkness . . 98
   Little flock and great world 102

FOREWORD

Six years after the promulgation of the conciliar constitution *Gaudium et Spes* (On the Church in the Modern World), Hans Urs von Balthasar published this programmatic little book under its original title *In Gottes Einsatz leben*.[1] Both texts aim to set forth an understanding of the role of the Church in the world. Both appreciate that a dynamic program of openness to the world is an exigence flowing from her missionary nature. Indeed, in the years leading up to the Council, von Balthasar had been urging the Church to dismantle the barriers protecting her from the world, precisely in order that the Church be free to fulfill her mission. In an earlier (and equally programmatic) work, *Razing the Bastions*, von Balthasar had called for "an ever deeper and more serious incarnation" of the Church in the world.[2] Since the Church exists to bring the salvation of Christ to all, he had argued, she must follow Christ's path of "descent" into the world and assume Christ's form of life. This entails acting and suffering for the sake of "the least" among us (Mt 25:40) and bearing responsibility in and with Christ for the destiny of all.

Yet while the Council Fathers in *Gaudium et Spes* enter into dialogue with the whole of humanity, recommending measures for the building up of society in the light of the

---

[1] *In Gottes Einsatz leben* (Einsiedeln: Johannes Verlag, 1971). English translation: *Engagement with God* (San Francisco: Ignatius Press, 2008). Henceforth *EWG*.

[2] *Razing the Bastions* (San Francisco: Ignatius Press, 1993) p. 71. German original: *Schleifung der Bastionen* (Einsiedeln: Johannes Verlag, 1952).

Gospel, von Balthasar here sets forth "a discourse *ad intra*, within the Church".[3] This inward turn on his part does not signify a turning away from the world. Such a reversal he could only regard as a desertion of the Christian mission. Rather, von Balthasar speaks chiefly to the Christian for the purpose of priming him to be an effective and credible instrument of God's involvement in the world. This preparation requires above all a reflection on the indispensable elements of Christianity. "Every program of mission to the world", he insists, "must at all times contain what Guardini called 'the discernment of what is Christian'."[4]

As in most of his works, so also here von Balthasar directs our gaze to the figure of Christ crucified. In beholding him, the discerning eye seizes on "the whole essence" of the Christian faith: "that we should understand that the love that characterizes the life of the Trinity has been manifested in [Christ], and in him has been *abundantly* proved."[5] Abundantly, indeed. For von Balthasar, the hallmark of the true God, that which renders the mission of Christ wholly credible as *God's* definitive engagement with the world, is love that radiates the quality of "excess", the "ever greater", the "yet more". *Deus semper major*. In the face of the recklessly self-forgetful character of God's crucified love, the only appropriate response is summed up in the Ignatian motto "*ad majorem Dei gloriam*", and in the Johannine exhortation, "so we ought to lay down our lives for our brothers" (I Jn 3:16). The more the Christian grasps the lengths to which the triune God involves himself for us, the greater grows his own ambition to live no longer for himself.

[3] *My Work in Retrospect* (San Francisco: Ignatius Press, 1993) p. 103. Henceforth *MWR*.
[4] *MWR*, p. 52.
[5] *EWG*, p. 41. My italics.

This means, to be sure, that the form and measure of
God's action in Christ provides the model for Christian
action. Von Balthasar, however, is acutely aware that something more is involved. If Christian action is to be *effective*
as a sign and instrument of God's saving love, it is not enough
to attempt to imitate the God of Jesus Christ by standing in
solidarity with the poor, the stranger, and the oppressed.
Neither the life of the Trinity nor the life of Christ is to be
regarded as a mere paradigm to guide programs of social
and political involvement. The crucial factor is that Christian action *participates in* the absolute freedom of God's interpersonal love. Christ, through his Incarnation and the
bestowal of his Spirit, imparts to us a participation in the
infinite freedom of his divine Sonship, by virtue of which
we are made capable of taking part in his trinitarian mission. Hence the significance and success of our openness to
the world depends upon the Trinity's prior opening of its
sphere of divine freedom to our participation. "Only if we
start from this 'Alpha' will our involvement lead us to the
'Omega'",[6] that is, to mankind's ever greater destiny of solidarity in God as "sons in the Son".

One of the outstanding merits of this little book emerges
from these observations. Without taking up a polemical
stance, it is equipped to perform a prophetic and critical
function against a "secularization of salvation". All that it
affirms about God's revelation in Christ as "an invitation
into the realm of . . . divine freedom" [7] is pregnant with the
insight that the transformation God intends to effect in us
is nothing less than "divinization". By rousing the Christian consciousness to a renewed awareness that man's full

[6] Ibid., p. 40.
[7] Ibid., p. 6.

and final liberation coincides with his "divinization", von Balthasar enables us "to judge clearly how basically unsatisfying it is for man ... to have as his ultimate goal the civilizing and humanizing of the world".[8]

Another of the book's virtues is that its "program of mission to the world" eliminates the false dichotomy between action and contemplation. According to von Balthasar, Christian action derives from and is sustained by contemplation, even as contemplation has its source in action: for "[w]hat we are looking at when we contemplate the love of God is 'Christ *giving* himself in love'".[9] In contemplating this, God's active involvement, we are spurred to play our part in the action.

A further gain is that *Engagement with God* can serve as an introduction to the second part of von Balthasar's massive theological trilogy: *Theo-drama: Theological Dramatic Theory*.[10] In non-technical language he broadly sketches some themes that are central to and developed at length in *Theo-drama*. Here we can note only a few that highlight the form of Christ's mission to the world. Christ reveals the essence of true freedom in being obedient "even unto death" (Phil 2:8). Christ discloses the nature of true power in letting himself be rendered powerless as a function of boundless love. In Christ we encounter a love sufficiently free to hand itself over to the autonomy of the other, a love sufficiently powerful to endure to the end the forces hostile to love. Indeed with Christ it is a case—the unique case—of love human and divine, without confusion or separation, bearing God-forsakenness in atonement for sin, once and for all

[8] Ibid., p. 69.

[9] Ibid., p. 47. My italics.

[10] *Theo-drama: Theological Dramatic Theory* in 5 volumes (San Francisco: Ignatius Press, 1988–1998).

(1 Jn 2:2; 4:10). Christ unveils, finally, the fulfillment of human freedom in being raised bodily from the dead and returning home "to the open spaces of divine freedom" in the bosom of his Father. Thereby Christ proves that he is "the very embodiment of God's mighty act of liberation".[11]

All this bears upon the *credibility* of the Christian's engagement. "For as Christ of his free love yielded himself willingly ... to death, and dereliction,"[12] so the Christian is called to be at God's disposal in readiness to serve his brothers and sisters without counting the cost. The credibility of Christian action as an engagement with *God* for the sake of the world resides in its grace-engendered likeness to "the foolishness" of divine love (1 Cor 1:25). Only this form of life "can penetrate the 'secular world' as 'leaven'."[13] The costly discipleship that hazards everything is the mark of authentic Christian involvement.

Von Balthasar anticipates our protests. "It will be objected that such a program of action demands the character of a saint. This may well be; but from the very beginning, Christian living has always been most credible, where at the very least it has shown a few faint signs of true holiness."[14]

Margaret M. Turek

St. Patrick's Seminary and University
Feast of St. Patrick
March 17, 2008

---

[11] *EWG*, p. 27.
[12] Ibid., pp. 27–28.
[13] *MRW*, p. 57.
[14] *EWG*, p. 61.

TRANSLATOR'S NOTE

I am most grateful to the author for being given the opportunity, through the kindness of the editors of S.P.C.K., to translate this important and profound book. I would also like to express my indebtedness to Mrs. Margaret Hollis for her help in revising my translation; and to the author himself for his careful correction of some passages in the translation.

R.J.H.

PREFACE

The world of today, when faced with the Christian Church, is filled with a sense of profound mistrust. Strangely enough, this lack of trust has increased rather than decreased since Vatican Council II, which, having stressed the very intimate relevance of the Church to the world as part of its program, summoned the Church to involve herself wholeheartedly in the care of the modern world. The reason for this lack of trust, however, is probably that people are no longer making any headway with humanistically inspired plans of action—there are enough of these to be found in political movements of all kinds. They are more prone to put their faith in the kind of activity that effectively changes the world, whatever the ideological background to this may be. Should, therefore, the Christian Church be of the opinion that only the Christian religion is able to inspire an appropriately planned course of activity of this sort, then she would be likely to speak of a hidden presence of "grace", to be discerned wherever men acted in this way, and to describe a man engaged in such activities as an "anonymous Christian". God's purpose after all was not merely to redeem the Church, but to save the world; the grace that he has bestowed upon the world in Jesus Christ must of necessity flood over the boundaries of the visible Church, even though the Church continues to be seen as a kind of focal point of grace, the *sacramentum mundi*, as she has been called by the Council. There is nothing new, of course, in this point of view. For centuries now, theology has spoken of a "baptism by desire" (*in voto*), that is, a baptism received by those who according to their limited insights have resolutely involved themselves in the kind of activity that contributes most to the welfare of their fellow men and of the world as a whole. These men are received and sustained by God's grace and are made invisible members of the visible Church.

Such a view is no doubt liberating for many, and it is certainly not our intention here to call it in question or to return to an earlier and narrower interpretation of the saying "Outside the Church there is no salvation." We ourselves support that new and more generous exegesis of the phrase, believing that God's grace is bestowed in every part of the world because the "whole Christ" fills the world with his presence—Christ, who is eternally and inseparably both Head and Body, the man from Nazareth raised to the dignity of Lord, and the community that draws its life from him, his Church insofar as she possesses his Spirit and follows his example.

Such an interpretation, however, has its hazards. It does indeed point to the fact that the Church at heart stands open to the world. But it creates the impression, particularly for those outside the Church, that the visible Church is nothing more than an institution, burdened with a quantity of rules, laws, and precepts as to what is to be believed and how life is to be conducted, whereas the very essence of the life of this institution can equally well be found outside its walls, scattered all over the world. And the driving forces of the institutional Church, for example, her hierarchical organization, her rules about Sunday worship and the reception of the sacraments, and, more incisively, the rules regulating married life, if taken in isolation, appear lacking in credibility, superfluous, disturbing, and even directly opposed to the life and example of Christ. In fact, if the actual essence of Christianity is disseminated throughout the entire human race, then the "Church of Christ" is left with but the form or carcass of Christianity as its distinguishing feature. Once this point of view has become prevalent—and it has to a great extent—then the Church is going to be hard put to escape being classified in this way; she will see herself as essentially an "organization" whose function is merely to organize the transmission of the light of Christianity, which issues from her and floods out into the world. This was certainly the image that predominated in the movement known as Catholic Action, launched in the early twentieth century, though it has now ceased to exist in most countries and in others is destined for extinction. But how otherwise then is the Church to see herself, once the theory of "anonymous Christians" is accepted, the theory, that is to say, that all men who struggle for the salvation and advancement of the human race in the spirit of self-sacrificing activity are united together in a living, quasi-religious union? Has the Church still a function to fulfill that is more than that of being a mere functionary in this process? There are indeed quite enough Bibles printed for everyone who has the inclination to acquaint himself with the life and work of Jesus and his disciples, without a particular social organization announcing that it has exclusive rights over the contents of the book. Today at face value at least, in any case in the West, that is the dilemma, and the questions this raises are not easy to answer. For the more liberally the Church is opened up to the world and accepts its values, bathing them in a Christian light, the more it seems that all that is left to the Church is the purely formal, which robs her of her credibility. From all sides, therefore, her outward structure is attacked, even in places where Christian values are still, to a certain extent, accepted.

It is possible, however, that this dilemma that looms so large in our immediate relationship with the Church is not so inexorable as it first appears. We have only to look East, to men such as the great Christian writers of Russia, Solzhenitsyn, Daniel Sinjawski, Michael Bulgakov, and others, or to the Baptist movement in Russia, to see something quite new. The practical aspects of the problem are transferred to a different sphere altogether. Here there are still some traces remaining of the hierarchical and liturgical life of the Church, which is constantly under threat, though tolerated to a certain extent. The opponents of Christianity do not direct the main force of their attack against this, but rather against people and groups of people who are living a distinctively Christian life. And it is more their way of life that is attacked than the things they say. It is indeed strange that in the writings of Solzhenitsyn, self-confessed Christians are basically peripheral characters and apparently play no decisive part in the plot. On the other hand, however, the landscape of humanity, painted for us in all its fearsome and tragic colors, is lit by a glow of reconciliation that one cannot specifically designate as "Christian", but which in an almost inexplicable manner brings this estranged world back to reality. The ideologies behind which men hide fall away like scales, to leave their true faces unmasked (as in the novel *Cancer Ward*), the harsh glare of the searchlights is extinguished, and things appear once more as they fundamentally are, without any attempt at pretense. In this, the contradiction that we formerly noted between life and institution has been transcended. For it is precisely this "anonymous light" of Christianity that lights up all places and all characters, unique, unparalleled, penetrating, that irritates

the ideologists and stirs them up to persecute and fight for
its extermination. Can anyone forbid this light to shine? Is
it possible that Pontius Pilate could sentence the risen Christ
to death a second time, Christ who has had the impertinence
to go on living? He is indeed no mere phantom: "Handle
me and see;" he says, "for a spirit has not flesh and bones
as you see that I have" [Lk 24:39]; but, in spite of this, he
himself cannot be crucified afresh, nor can he be beaten
with rods.

The disciples of this Jesus, however, who can indeed be
beaten with rods, have nonetheless inherited something of
this secret. They are, it is true, "organized" insofar as they
are organically linked together and constitute a Church, but
whoever directs his attack at their organization will not, in
fact, touch them. For they are brothers to all those who in
this world are involved in the struggle for human rights,
but those who claim that they are simply a particular kind
of humanist (or "anonymous Christian") have once more
failed to do them justice. They have a clear and irritating
way of making themselves distinct (for why otherwise would
Solzhenitsyn or Sinjawski have been persecuted in such a
way?), which is not simply to be identified with the fact
that they are members of a religious union. They, and many
others of their kind who are less conspicuous, are lights in
the world; and the theme of the pages that follow is to ask
ourselves the question, what is this power or this brilliant
light, from where does it derive, and what is the connection between the source of power that nourishes the Christian and his involvement with mankind?

One thing we can say immediately is that from the true
Christian there radiates the kind of freedom that is constantly only being sought after by the non-Christian. In modern times, the freedom of man is a theme that preoccupies

both Christian and non-Christian, and a competition is in process as to who can understand this freedom more profoundly, who more effectively put it into practice. Atheistic philosophies are wholly taken up with this preoccupation. The Enlightenment was concerned with the freeing of reason from the fetters of faith; Marx wrote of the freeing of economically enslaved man in order that he may undertake work suited to his dignity; Freud wrote of the freeing of the individual from the bondage of a past as yet unmastered; Nietzsche spoke of the rescuing of the whole of mankind from the nightmare of a concept (namely, God) that is no longer believed in and which has been dragged along like a corpse through world history. Everywhere at the very portals of freedom, man seems to be chained to some past, to a traditional custom, to a moment in history made absolute, or to some forbidden totem in the realm of nature or civilization. And yet he becomes truly man only when he has chosen himself in freedom and consummated himself, when the "nature" in him has been totally and freely appropriated and responsibly permeated. So long as Christianity is seen to be principally a matter of traditions and institutions, other contemporary movements toward freedom will have no difficulties. The competition will begin in earnest only when the Christian undertakes to show in theory that God's free revelation of himself in Jesus Christ is an invitation into the realm of an absolute and divine freedom, in which alone human freedom can be fully realized. Nor is this just an invitation, but through God's becoming man in Jesus Christ, which is an example to all of true fulfillment, there is a breakthrough and entry into the sphere of precisely that kind of freedom which is so feverishly sought after by modern man but which, without the revelation of God, he can never otherwise find. As opposed to those whose search for freedom urges them onward into a barren void, the Christian stands as the messenger of freedom accomplished and a freedom attainable by all. Notwithstanding, he must be careful not to overlook a weighty objection that is levelled against his standpoint as it is against the position of a well-founded kind of modern evolutionism. We live in a world, it is said, that from time immemorial has advanced by means of the aggressiveness of the strong and the destruction of the weak, whose every "good" movement is founded on the principle of "exploitation" and "suppression" on the part of the "so-called evil" (O. Lorenz). How can such a world advance toward freedom; how is even the merest preliminary sketch of freedom thinkable? At all events, this worldview, which can scarcely be dismissed as unscientific, resists all theories, be they Marxist or Christian, that dream of the rise of a kingdom of peace on earth, set up in the name of Lenin or Christ. Were there then capitalism and exploitation in the world before man made his appearance? Many biologists who were unwilling to renounce this view were sent to Siberia after the Communists had seized power. But is not a world based on such principles quite unacceptable for us Christians also as a basis for Christian teaching? Is a world like this the work of a good God? Is it capable of being transformed, or are we to say that whoever opposes this world in the name of Christ and freedom is not in fact destined to be sold ruthlessly to destruction? Are perhaps Christians and Communists alike Utopian in their efforts to find freedom? Have perhaps the Christians only this advantage, that nourished by a source which lies beyond the limits of this world, they can, with their Utopian hope, reach out toward a goal that lies beyond the boundaries of time? And that it is their movement which provides the one glimmer of the light of freedom in a world of murder and senselessness?

PART ONE

THE DIVINE INVOLVEMENT

To begin with, we have been looking at a dilemma, tragic as it is unproductive, that is unfortunately still of real consequence for us today. We have also hinted at a way of escaping from this dilemma, and it remains for us now to bring our original premonitions under closer scrutiny. The object of our quest is to find a way of overcoming the dualism that exists between the Church and the world. This will not be achieved by simply declaring that this is in fact a nonexistent dualism. Rather the distinction must be set out in such a way as to allow the union we are striving after to be a genuine union when it does take place. The parable of the leaven provides a suitable point of departure. The dough to be made into bread is a lifeless lump of dull, inedible matter; but the yeast, too, is by itself completely inedible, despite the fact that it is the principle whereby the lump is to be turned into bread fit to eat. The yeast must be plunged into the dough; it must sink into it and disappear, in order that its energy may be released and the dough transformed into bread. Alone, it is nothing; buried in the dough it is quite the opposite. But, note, separateness, and indeed a strict separateness, is the preliminary to the unity that is being attempted and that alone will result in something palatable. The yeast must by itself go through several stages of processing before it can be fully effective. Only then is it economical to use it and bury it in the three measures of meal in which its effectiveness can be realized. Now the question before us is, what is it that makes the Christian like leaven, what gives him the power to be a leavening in the world? What is it that gives him a special quality for which nothing else can substitute? Now in asking what "gives" him, we have reached a point of crucial importance. For he cannot by himself take what it is that makes him a Christian; it must be *given* to him; and this gift to him is grace. We must remember, of course, that he must take this gift and make it his own; for, at the beginning, he too is but dough that must undergo a thorough mixing before it becomes leaven. Grace, however, is not just a vague force from outside or from above; in history, grace has a quite special character, which is already beginning to be delineated in the Old Testament and reaches its final form in the New. It is therefore quite indispensable that we should begin by saying something about the character of grace in order that from this we can go on to define the character of the Christian who in turn, for his part, will help to form the true character of the world.

THE MEANING OF THE OLD TESTAMENT

God's Involvement in Choosing

All ancient peoples have their gods. The God of Israel, however, is distinguished from all other gods by the fact that he brings into being a people to worship him by his own free sovereign act of choosing—whether we look at the first manifestation of this choice of a people—when God called Abraham—or at his choosing his people when he led them out of Egypt at the hand of Moses (who himself had first to be called of God), thus making something like a nation out of a miserable collection of uncultured and demoralized slaves; before all this, in each case there is a free act of the divine initiative that can neither be foreseen, demanded, nor deduced. The choosing of the whole people of God can be traced back only as far as the patriarchs who received an initial promise. This choice, however, is not governed by any obvious principle.

> "It was not because you were more in number than any other people that the LORD set his love upon you and chose you, for you were the fewest of all peoples; but it is because the LORD loves you, and is keeping the oath which he swore to your fathers, that the LORD has brought you out with a

mighty hand, and redeemed you from the house of bondage" (Deut 7:7–8).

It is true that, later, Israel set her calling within a wider
frame of reference, when she began to suspect that she
had not been called for her own sake, but in order that
she might be a leaven in the world. Then it was that she
inserted the covenant with Noah before the covenant with
Abraham and Moses, as representing the peace concluded
between God and the whole created order and all men in
human history. By doing this, Israel recognized the true
role she was called to play. It never occurred to her, however, to take a relativist attitude toward her role and to see
the covenant with Abraham and that on Sinai as more tran-
sient manifestations of the general covenant between God
and man. In the Christian era, the Fathers, St. Augustine
in particular, were to express the view that the *civitas Dei*,
the polity or city of God, among men was in existence
from the very beginning of the human race, but they do
not thereby deny that the meaningful center of this presence of God in the world was to begin with Israel, and,
after Christ, has been the Church of the New Covenant.
For as Israel could only view the covenant with Noah in
the light of the covenant with Abraham and the covenant
on Sinai, so too Augustine could only discern the presence and nature of the *civitas Dei* in the light of Christ
himself.

The free choice and initiative of a God who is ever free
always constitutes the concrete form under which grace is
manifested among men. We could say that this unfathom-
able sovereign act of God robes him in the character of
a despotic potentate and degrades man to the status of a
slave, condemned to a life of mere obedience. This free

choosing, however, is not primarily a manifestation of power but a revelation of love. The text that we have just quoted bears this out. And if this act of God in choosing is first and foremost an act of boundless love, then the response expected and indeed required by such love is certainly a gentle obedient Yes of submission and willingness to comply, but from the beginning a simple return of love in gratitude for love given. But the response is nonetheless one of obedience. God will bring his people out of Egypt, make them pass through the Red Sea, destroy their persecutors, give them food and drink in a wonderful manner in the wilderness, and God himself will go before them and as a pillar of cloud and a pillar of fire mark the places where they are to rest. Wherever the cloud descends, there must the people pitch their tents; when it rises again, the people must break camp and march on, always following the God who leads. It is inconceivable that Israel should ever take over the leadership and that God should follow behind his people. For what is first required of Israel is that she should obey and live in harmony with the ways of the God who has chosen her. At the same time, however, she knows that what God does effects her freedom and that the fact that he has liberated her from the slavery of Egypt cannot mean that she is to be brought into a new slavery to Yahweh. She knows rather that she has been liberated in order that, through her following of the God of liberty, she may enter upon a freedom that is truly her own. The foundation of her choosing, which is God's innate freedom, must correspond with the ultimate purpose of her choosing, namely, that she may participate in the liberty of God himself. Hence all obedience serves as a preparation for freedom. The text "Be holy, as I am holy" means (if we understand it correctly) "Be free, even as I am free" (but at what sacrifices must such an understanding be purchased!).

The desacralization that begins in the Old Testament and is fully consummated in the New is a liberation (of men) from the sacrality of the cosmos and from its powers to the point where man himself appears as "holy" in his act of committing himself freely to the perfect freedom of God. Slavery now lies behind us; that is the point of departure. Perfect freedom lies ahead of us; that is our eschatological goal. Certainly, the people of the Old Covenant know that God is a God of power; yet it is just this power which frees them from slavery. They know, moreover, that his power is his love, which demands my love in return, and that love can only be given freely. "Hear O Israel: The LORD our God is one LORD; and you shall love the LORD your God with all your heart, and with all your soul, and with all your might" (Deut 6:4–5). That is the archetypal situation that will never become a mere fact of past history. This is the living source from which we must never withdraw. These premises must never be forgotten when— and precisely when—the inferences are being worked out. For our freedom is inseparable from the fact that we have been made free.

> "And when the LORD your God brings you into the land which he swore to your fathers, to Abraham, to Isaac, and to Jacob, to give you, with great and excellent cities, which you did not build, and houses full of good things, which you did not fill, and cisterns hewn out, which you did not hew, and vineyards and olive trees, which you did not plant, and when you eat and are full, then take heed lest you forget the LORD, who brought you out of the land of Egypt, out of the house of bondage" (Deut 6:10–12).

We shall find again and again that obedience to God is the underlying motive in every act initiated by man, an obedience, moreover, that is always demanded suddenly, out of the blue, and that has constantly to be put into practice. The testing of King Saul is an event that, at first sight, almost defies our comprehension. Before going into battle against the Philistines, he is obliged to wait for Samuel, who is to offer a burnt sacrifice. Samuel fails to arrive on the appointed day; the enemy attacks, and the army is already in disarray when, at the last minute, Saul himself offers the sacrifice. For this action, he is deposed by God, for God requires obedience, and not sacrifice (see 1 Sam 13:8ff.; 15:22). This condemnation applies not only to the use of sacrifice, but also to the use of elementary political cunning, as we can see in the similar case of Hezekiah, who, being forbidden by the prophet Isaiah to offer resistance to the Assyrians, encamped before Jerusalem, saved the city by his obedience and not by military tactics (Is 36). In a similar situation, Jeremiah warns King Zedekiah against rebelling against the supremacy of Babylon (Jer 27—29), but the king prefers to rely on his political expertise and seeks an alliance with the Egyptians (which Jeremiah knew would be fruitless; see Jer 37:7–8). He makes an unsuccessful attempt to escape when the city is taken, and after witnessing the murder of his children, he is blinded and carried away to Babylon. These are but a few examples that illustrate the theology of history of the Deuteronomists, who together trace a single theme through Israel's history. Their theme is the story of Israel's obedience to the Lord of the Covenant, through following his clear guidance, of her turning away her heart from God, of her punishment, conversion, and final salvation at the hand of God. For to think we know better how to fight our way to freedom by ourselves, leads us inevitably back into the bondage of Egypt (see Hos 9:1–3).

The Chosen

We must now ask who it is that is chosen by God. Is it an individual or does God choose a whole people? A glance at the history of Israel shows us that this is a difficult question to answer. Central to God's plan is indeed the choosing of a people. The covenant at Sinai is made between God and his people; Moses is merely its visible executor and mediator. And at the end of the Book of Joshua, the people are very solemnly asked to choose, during the election at Shechem, whether they seriously wish to ratify the covenant with God or to serve other gods. Joshua warns the people against treating this matter lightheartedly,

> "for he is a holy God; he is a jealous God; he will not forgive your transgressions or your sins. . . . And the people said to Joshua, 'No; but we will serve the LORD.' . . . So Joshua made a covenant with the people that day, and made statutes and ordinances for them at Shechem" (Josh 24:19, 21, 25).

Hence it is with the community that God enters into covenant.

It must not be overlooked, however, that every aspect of this covenant with the community rests on the relationship of God to certain specially chosen individuals. A necessary preliminary to the covenant at Sinai is the covenant relationship of mutual trust made between God and the patriarchs. Everything begins with the personal relationship established in solitude between God and Abraham; and in the theology of St. Paul and St. James, Abraham, on account of his own personal faith (which, when he offers the son of promise in sacrifice, has to be a blind act of faithful obedience) is destined to become the father of all faithful people, be they Jews or Gentiles. The individual must allow himself to be led "whither he would not" and the people must follow him in order that they may be sharers in the promise he has received. The Exodus from Egypt would have been inconceivable had not Moses first been called; for it is only with Moses that God speaks "face to face, as a man speaks to his friend" (Ex 33:11): "With him I speak mouth to mouth, clearly and not in dark speech; and he beholds the form of the LORD" (Num 12:8). In all his words and actions, Moses is himself the embodiment of the whole people in the sight of God and is therefore able at God's behest to represent God to the people. The same situation recurs in the time of David, the "king after God's heart". The messianic promise is to be the peculiar possession of David and his house; but even then, when God will eventually assume in person the role of shepherd and savior of his people and seal the final "covenant of peace", he will do so in the person of a single shepherd, "my servant David" (Ezek 34:25, 24).

Having said this, we cannot as yet determine whether the principle of community or the principle of individuality is the more fundamental nor which deserves greater priority. For we can neither say that the community is only a collection of isolated individuals, for it is rather by its very nature genuinely conscious of itself as the subject of God's choosing and aware of being led by him to salvation. Nor can one say that the chosen individual, be he patriarch or leader of his people, judge, king, or prophet, is the real partner with God in the covenant, while the people of God are merely tolerated as so many appendages of the person who represents them. For these individuals who tower above the rest only hold their office and status with reference to the community that they both serve and represent.

At this point we can now already look ahead to the New Testament. Here the individual and the community become, if possible, yet more inseparable and mutually interrelated. In the Old Testament, the people still constitute an ethnic community whose statutory ordinances at times can function without the momentum provided by a particular person (as does the hereditary priesthood). In the New Testament this will no longer be possible, because the Church, being the fullness of Jesus Christ, will proceed out of his person (*Ecclesia ex latere Christi*), whereas on the other hand, Jesus, in his manhood, proceeds out of the person of his Mother, who in her total obedience and unswerving faith will become the real type and abiding center of the Church, the bride of Christ. For it is precisely in the relationship between Christ and Mary and between Christ and the Church that the circle that links both the individual and the community becomes incapable of dissolution. But we must first bring to an end our discussion of the Old Testament foundations.

The Encounter between the Chooser and the Chosen

As we saw, the reason for God's choosing man lies in his love, free and groundless. It promotes as response the free, reciprocal love of the chosen, because free love can only be answered with love given freely. Therefore the love of God requires of those whom he chooses a free return of love.

This must always be borne in mind when considering the "commandments" and "laws" of the Old Testament. After all, in the final analysis the tone of these is "may" rather than "must" (since they are directed to those living close to the presence of God). They are laws that reflect that closeness and intimacy that one would expect to find consequent upon a covenant of love. "[Y]ou shall therefore be holy, for I am holy" (Lev 11:45; 19:2; see 20:26). The very closeness and intimacy of Israel to the realm of the divine makes of her "a kingdom of priests and a holy nation" (Ex 19:6), for she is "his own possession" (see Lev 20:26; Deut 7:6; 26:18). Again, this collective holiness is closely related to personal holiness, which is demanded of each one individually. For all those who personally remain close to the presence of God are as individuals accounted "holy" (see Ps 17:3; 34:10, 18). Central to this concept of holiness in the Book of Deuteronomy is the demand that love shall be undivided. The heart of this last book of the Mosaic law originates in the Northern Kingdom in the time of the prophet Hosea, who is responsible for the boldest utterances about the compassionate love of God toward Israel, even when she had sinned. Already in Israel the acute emphasis on the strict keeping of the Commandments signifies nothing less than the first fruits of her love expressed in actions. In all this it is relatively unimportant that Israel only later came to understand and express her demonstration of loyalty to the covenant as love, since for men of those early days, loyalty (or righteous behavior in accordance with the covenant: *zedek*) was the only proper expression of love and, moreover, her loyalty to the covenant is effected wholly and entirely by the loving kindness (*chesed*) and grace of God that goes before. The Commandments, therefore, which in their breadth of compass are made to range over many aspects of human nature and human existence, are, according to this understanding, simply the means whereby it is made possible for men to be led into freedom from their bondage to the powers of this world. By means of the Commandments, the order of nature, built to a considerable extent on the principle of aggression and ethically unordered, becomes, so to speak, ethically ordered (*ethizesthai*, as Aristotle would say). Thus it is led out from the "Egypt" where it has lain in bondage to the laws of the subhuman creation into the realm of the truly human; and to be truly human involves loving and following the God who brings liberty. Each law therefore is a signpost on the eventful journey toward liberty.

Now the setting of man's activity, especially under the covenant, is the community in the context of which all of man's action and behavior takes place. It would be impossible to conceive of man maintaining a so-to-speak vertical and religious relationship toward God within the terms of the covenant and of his adopting a quite different law of behavior toward his fellow men that we might call horizontal and ethical. For this reason, on the two tables of the Law the Commandments concerning man's relationship to God (and those concerning the worship of God are followed closely by the laws and prescriptions relating to the ordering of the cult) pass straight on to those concerning his relationship to his neighbor. This is due to the fundamental fact that God makes his covenant as directly with the people as a whole as he does with the individual by himself, and that therefore the individual stands as directly within the covenant relationship when dealing with God as he does when he has to do with his fellow men. The connection, however, is closer than this, and this comes out most clearly when the Israelite has to deal with someone who is suffering under oppression or who has been deprived of his rights. On occasions like these, he has to think back to his own origins: "You have been liberated yourself; therefore act as a free man and be yourself a liberator." To God he owes his very being, so it is written on the first table of the Law. On the second, his sense of indebtedness is given practical expression in the social, political, and legal sphere of man's existence.

"Love the sojourner therefore; for you were sojourners in the land of Egypt" (Deut 10:19; cf. Ex 22:21; 23:9).

"If there is among you a poor man ... you shall not harden your heart.... If your brother, a Hebrew man, or a Hebrew woman, is sold to you, he shall serve you six years, and in the seventh year you shall let him go free from you. And when you let him go free from you, you shall not let him go empty-handed; you shall furnish him liberally out of your flock, out of your threshing floor, and out of your wine press.... You shall remember that you were a slave in the land of Egypt, and the LORD your God redeemed you" (Deut 15:7, 12–13, 15).

"You shall not oppress a hired servant who is poor and needy, whether he is one of your brethren or one of the sojourners ... ; you shall give him his hire on the day he earns it.... [Y]ou shall remember that you were a slave in Egypt and the LORD your God redeemed you from there; therefore I command you to do this. When you reap your harvest in your field, and have forgotten a sheaf in the field, you shall not go back to get it; it shall be for the sojourner, the fatherless, and the widow.... When you beat your olive trees, you shall not go over the boughs again; it shall be for the sojourner, the fatherless, and the widow. When you gather the grapes of your vineyard, you shall not glean it afterward; it shall be for the sojourner, the fatherless, and the widow. You shall remember that you were a slave in

the land of Egypt; therefore I command you to do this"
(Deut 24:14–15, 18–22).

This continual reiteration of the same principle helps us to
see that Jesus, in the parable of the unmerciful servant, was
simply summing up once for all in a simple portrait the very
heart of the Old Testament covenant law. Religion, after all,
is of necessity the mainspring of morality; for religion in the
Old Testament does not so much concern my behavior toward
God, but God's entering into a relationship with me. His act
of making me free is the foundation of everything, and this
everything includes both me and my people, my relationship to God, and my relationship to the world. There is no
question here of any tension. The love that God bestows on
me makes me become what I truly am, and what I will eventually be. It makes the "I" become the self, the real person
that God wants to see and desires to possess. For this love of
God in choosing us transforms the rather indeterminate "subject" or "individual" (which man would otherwise be, left
to his own devices) into a person in all senses unique. God
after all is simply unique, and by the act of choosing me by
a love that is unique, he makes me similarly unique in the
light of his love. At first every member of Israel is unique in
this sense. As one might expect, however, the behavior of
the people singled out by God's love makes itself felt, almost
imperceptibly for the time being, beyond the strict limits of
the chosen people of God. My behavior toward all other
people, even toward strangers is conditioned by this knowledge that I am unique, for it is this that establishes me as a
person and shows itself in all actions for which I am responsible. Later we shall see that this behavior can only be prop-
erly maintained if man in his actions remains true to the
principles by which he is constituted.

2

THE MEANING OF THE NEW COVENANT

Jesus as God's Involvement

The Old Covenant afforded us a superlatively clear picture of the God who chooses freely and of man, chosen that he might be free. It showed us their meeting and engaging with one another in a relationship of grace and obedience, of love given and love returned; and that this return of love determines the whole man in his religious, ethical, devotional, and secular existence. If we look now at the New Testament and say that the divine involvement reaches its consummation in the man, Jesus of Nazareth, does not then the whole scheme we have just outlined threaten to concertina? For in Jesus of Nazareth, God's word to us becomes simultaneously man's response to him, the God who chooses becomes mingled with man who is the object of this choice, and it is reasonable to fear that the ordered relationship of distance and proximity between God and man might become confused, that God might finally become totally absorbed in manhood and that man might then be able to consider himself endowed with the dignity of Godhood. It is a foolhardy risk that God takes in allowing his Word to "be made man" in Jesus, and it is because God is prepared to risk even the cross and the state of God-abandonment that Paul can speak of "the foolishness of God".

The fact that Jesus is the ultimate expression of the divine involvement is evident in a doctrine, central to primitive and, indeed, pre-Pauline Christianity and summed up in the phrase *pro nobis*—"on our behalf". "He who did not spare his own Son but gave him up for us all" [sharing our lost condition] (Rom 8:32). And the Son is not content to submit passively or unwillingly, for he takes on the Father's attitude of self-giving. "Christ died for our sins in accordance with the Scriptures, [and] ... he was buried" (1 Cor 15:3–4); "the Son of God ... loved me and gave himself for me" (Gal 2:20). The Son's devotion expressed the Father's condescension, which proves his overflowing love for the world (see Jn 3:16). One can next see this gesture simply as a radical expression of God's action in choosing that we saw in the Old Testament. Then this choosing was basically the means by which Israel was liberated from the "slavery of Egypt", and through which she became for the first time a real people. A people, however, possesses at least an element of freedom and autonomy; and by declaring Israel to be his own peculiar possession, God thus in advance liberates her from all other rulers, whether they be the kings of this world or angelic powers (see Deut 32:8). And in proportion as Israel denied the fact that she was God's own possession, so she forfeited this at the expense of her unique kind of freedom and became subject to some foreign power, suffering even the exile to Babylon and later in her history, subjection to Hellenistic princes and Roman emperors. God's final involvement in Jesus, however, results in effecting in man that final freedom which is described by both Paul (see Gal 5:1) and John (see Jn 8:32). This is freedom not only from political oppression, but from every kind of cosmic power: from fate, from the compelling lure of sin, from a state of estrangement from God, from the instinctive urge toward self-defense, aggression, and murder, from dissipation among all that is vain and futile, and finally from death itself. The effective working of all these forces is thereby crippled, rendered impotent, and destroyed (see 1 Cor 15:24–26). This, however, is only possible because these forces are conquered not from outside or from above, but from within by the process of God's "self-emptying" in the person of his Son, by his becoming obedient "even unto death", and (as the sign of Jonah prefigures) by his descending into the depths of the abyss, in order that man may not be left with any antidivine experience that God himself has not undergone, which he might count as peculiarly his own and use as a means of "getting back" at his Maker. It is necessary that all cosmic forces should be completely disarmed by God himself, in order that he may bring man, now liberated, back home to the open spaces of the divine freedom. Had Jesus in fact been *merely* a man, he would never have been able to have been himself the very embodiment of God's mighty act of liberation.

The fact that those freed by the divine action still live in the world does not mean that they belong to the world, as though possessed by the world and incorporated into its structure. They are indeed in themselves finite individuals, but are no longer in slavery for—through the process of dying and rising with Christ—they have broken through into the infinity and freedom of God himself. "But if Christ is in you, although your bodies are dead because of sin, your spirits are alive because of righteousness" (Rom 8:10). In these words Paul describes the essential freedom of the Christian, in the middle of his continuing solidarity with humanity that has fallen prey to death. For as Christ of his free love yielded himself willingly to be bound under obedience to fate, death, and dereliction, thereby breaking their compelling hold, so the Christian preserves a deep and inward freedom while continuing to live among these earthly powers and ordinances (see Mt 17:26; Gal 4:5; 1 Pet 2:16).

This mighty and quite unexpected act of God, who involved himself for the sake of mankind to the extent of his Word being made man and Jesus dying and being raised from the dead, signifies man's vocation to become what in truth he really is. He is called thereby to realize his own freedom, for man (in the final analysis) is simply what he chooses to be. For as Israel was "no people" before being called and liberated from Egypt (she was "no people"— 1 Pet 2:10, and as though she was a thing that did not exist— see Rom 4:17) and only constituted a living entity in the eyes of God after being called by him—so too the Christian, in his personal as in his social life, is not truly himself until he is within God's involvement in Jesus, by which he is rescued from his state of alienation where his "understanding lay darkened", and, being delivered from the "power of darkness", is brought into the clear light of self-knowledge that reveals to him his true identity, shows him his true vocation, and enlightens him as to the real meaning of his existence.

God's involvement of himself "on our behalf", therefore, does not consist of his making some external pronouncement of forgiveness (to use a forensic image) of which we are either unaware or only subsequently find applied to us (for so many would understand the process of justification). God's action impinges on us at a much deeper level, at the very heart of our being. For the grace of God is fundamentally a call; it is being enlisted in God's service; it is being commissioned with a special task; and through all this there is bestowed upon us a unique personal dignity in the eyes of God. We have yet to explain how this is so. Suffice to say here that our being chosen by God means (in a negative sense) being rescued from the clutches of the powers of this world and (in a positive sense) being appointed to a service, unique as it is personal, and being endowed with a spark of God's own uniqueness. Thereby, God enlists us as the agents of his activity in the world, takes us for his own, and gives us "a new name ... which no one knows except him who receives it" (Rev 2:17). For in proportion as God makes us free in ourselves, so we are correspondingly free and at his disposal for his activity in the world. St. Paul sees the Christian's freedom and his service in God's free work as two sides of the same coin (see Rom 6:15–23). And it is in the living out of this paradox of freedom and service that man comes to be most truly himself.

The Chosen

Under the Old Covenant Israel was the elect of God, chosen, however, not as a mere anonymous collection of people but given personal quality through its great representatives, in whose persons God looked upon the people as a whole, and whose duty it was to represent the people to God. Under the New Covenant, the individual/community tension is alleviated in two ways. To begin with, the many representatives of the people of old were all forerunners of the one, final, and effective representative of men to God. For Jesus himself is the elect of God; it is he who was promised, it is he who is Messiah, the anointed One, the Christ. Alone and unique, he is both Son of God and Son of Man; on both counts, his dignity and the task he is commissioned to fulfill are of universal significance, concerned with not just one people, but with all mankind. All men indeed live under the dominion of the powers of this world and are subject to death; but Jesus suffers in his own person our common bondage and fallenness and therefore represents all men to God. Henceforward each individual is looked upon by his heavenly Father in the light of the redeeming work of the Son. And it is precisely on account of this that the whole of humanity, seen by God in the Son, constitutes a unit. In Christ men find a common destiny; in him they constitute a new and universal Israel whose common bond is the Son's destiny that is decisive for every man.

We have, however, by no means exhausted this theme. In the Son's work, we see the Father's involvement of himself in love (see Jn 3:16; Rom 8:32) and the Son never ceases to remind us that he and his Father share in a common task, which itself is the revelation par excellence that the Godhead in fact is a community of Persons. It remains a unity no less when the distinction is made between the Father (who sends) and the Son (who is sent), a unity so absolute, however, that this unity in itself constitutes a third focus in the Godhead, namely, the Spirit, who comes at the very moment that the Son departs (see Jn 16:7), who is the Spirit of the Father (see Rom 8:11) as he is the Spirit of the Son (see Rom 8:9), whom the Father sends in the name of the Son (see Jn 14:26), and whom the Son sends from the Father (see Jn 15:26). It is in this sense that the involvement of this unique, free, and personal God is at the same time the involvement of the community of Persons that constitutes the divine society, and if we look at the structures of their involvement, we shall see that, in the realm of the Absolute, the principles of individuality and community are at work together simultaneously, so that the Person makes demands and imposes conditions on the community, and the community does likewise in respect of the Persons. For only in this sense can God in fact be "Love", without reference to any object of his love in this world. In the Godhead, therefore, individuality and community have a common origin, for here there exists so intimate a community that the Persons coinhere perfectly in one another; they constitute in fact a communion of the purest kind and are only distinct in order that the one may live for the sake of the other. Thus here the principle of individuality—the inviolable prerequisite for any full communion—totally excludes any idea of what we in a world of finite beings would call "private".

Through the Incarnation of the Son, however, a member of this heavenly society becomes a human being. This marks the beginning of human society being fashioned according to the spirit and form of the heavenly society. True, psychological and sociological principles of community living are not thereby excluded, but they are given a final point of reference that lies beyond their somewhat uncertain and precarious doctrines in God himself. In fact all earthly ordinances concerning personal life and interpersonal relationships have been objectively transcended since God in Christ totally involved himself, for the sake of the whole of humanity, in the sphere of the life of the Trinity. Saying that this in itself is objectively true does not yet mean that men acknowledge the subjective implications of this truth. For on the one hand, through the preaching of the gospel (Rom 10:14ff.), men will have to be confronted with this objective truth; yet on the other hand, when thus confronted they will have to ratify it in freedom or remain free to reject it out of hand. It is at this point, when we begin to see something of the dramatic nature of the history of our liberation, that the role of the *Church* becomes apparent.

Taking all things into consideration we see that the Church's role in the scheme of our salvation can only be a mediatorial yet dynamic one. She reenacts on a higher and universal level the part played by God's personal representatives among the people of Israel, that is, that of being the representative of God to the people and of the people to God. Under the New Covenant, this "people" is the whole of humanity. Hence the role of the Church in the world is not to be a kind of alternative society, shut off and enclosed, a community or society preoccupied with its own internal affairs, a spiritual "society of the perfect" that exists side by side with the secular order. The whole justification for her existence lies in her communicating to the rest of mankind the universally valid truths concerning God's liberating and redeeming work with fundamental openness, which in itself is but the continuation of God's involvement in Christ for the sake of the world. For this purpose, the Church only needs such visible structure as is necessary to permit her message and her genuineness to be proclaimed convincingly in the world. The question is, however, in what does this structure consist? It is built principally of men who have solidly affirmed their faith in God's total involvement in the work of liberating the world and have given it their full assent; in the act of believing, they lay hold of the reality of their liberation and seek to realize this in their own lives. Their faith leads them to submit to incorporation (by baptism) into that society offered by God to the world. This done, they take part in the mystery of the Eucharist, which mystery is itself but the total involvement of God himself. Here the Father offers to us his Son under the form of his supreme action on our behalf, giving us his flesh and his blood outpoured for our sustenance. They share, too, in a forgiveness of sins that is constantly renewed by the sacrament of conversion (or penance); they partake of the Holy Spirit, which fills the divine society. There is a ministry in the Church that exists to exercise a stewardship of these mysteries of God's gift of himself to the faithful. It is a service rendered to those who serve, a ministry of reconciliation toward those whose task it is to reconcile. It is in fact no more than this, nor should it be accorded any greater importance. It does, however, serve the function (as the Pauline Epistles show) of training people in that kind of obedience demanded by the Church and without which the Church would not be able to proclaim and witness convincingly to the obedience of Jesus to the Father. This obedience which the Church requires is a necessary factor, too, because the Church of necessity has, for the sake of the world, to reflect something of that absolute unity which characterizes the society of the divine Persons, in which nothing is private, where there are no divisions and no rivalries, but where the principle of unity is a love that encompasses and overrides all individuality. In the Church, therefore, each member is a person insofar as he assumes the unique role to which God by his grace has called him, in order that he may be truly a person, through serving the interests of the community as a whole. St. Paul's image of the Body and its many members illustrates this principle and has to stand the test of the most difficult situations (cf. Acts 21:17–30) and to hold good in the face of the almost disastrous tensions that arise from time to time between the "stronger" and the "weaker" brethren (see Rom 14–15; 1 Cor 8).

The Church, therefore, is Christ's fellow servant in his task of liberating the world. She shares with God in his work of sharing himself in Christ with the world. Hence the act of sharing must be at the very center of the Church's life and being. She can only be truly herself insofar as she accepts the fact that she is the means of God's sharing and imparting himself, and she can only fulfill her true nature in the process of distributing what she herself has been privileged to share in. St. Paul describes her as the Body of Christ, that Body which is actualized at the very place where Christ shares himself with those who share with him in the sacrificial meal (see 1 Cor 10:16ff.) and charges those who receive him to imitate his own disposition and willingness to share and to give (see 2 Cor 8–9). St. John draws the most obvious conclusion when he says that Christ "laid down his life for us; and we ought to lay down our lives for the brethren" (1 Jn 3:16). In the Church, therefore, there exists no other difference between the celebration of the sacraments and our everyday existence, save that between the source and its issue. Here, in the dynamic life of the Church and nowhere else, all the mysteries of our faith—the Trinity, the doctrine of the Person of Christ, the doctrines about the Church, the sacraments, the mystery of Christian living— come to be seen as nothing less than God's imparting of his life-giving love to us; and this love flows through the Church and out into the world.

Since God was made man there is no shorter way of answering the question as to who it is that under the New Covenant is the object of God's choosing than by stating the whole sequence—Christ, the Church, mankind; and we include under mankind, of course, the whole cosmos. All interpolations into this sequence must be regarded as purely relative or provisional; they are related to the final goal for which God has risked the whole of his involvement, that is, the world as a whole. "For God so loved the *world* . . ." (Jn 3:16, emphasis added). Indeed, from the

Christian point of view, the world is no longer an anonymous collection of individuals; for in proportion as the light
of heaven penetrates through Christ and the Church into
the darkness of the world, so it visibly gives personality to
the whole human community. Each man encountering this
light receives a call and a commission; to him is given the
task of living for others, and he becomes one of those who
have begun to grasp the meaning of communion and sharing. We are back once more to the parable of the leaven.
The dough that is as yet unleavened is a shapeless mass of
private existences that, because they are under the dominion of the powers of this world, are pushed together into a
collective lump. The leavening promises two things that cannot be seen in isolation: on the one hand, a release from
merely private existence in order that men may become
fully individual, and on the other hand, a release from collective existence for the sake of a genuine communion and
sharing.

The Encounter Between the Chooser
and the Chosen

We have perhaps moved too swiftly in our argument and
not taken sufficient notice of the yawning chasms that open
up all around us and obstruct the easy road to the synthesis
into which we have been attempting to resolve the involvement of God and the involvement of Christ. We must retrace
our steps a little and ponder the whole difficulty inherent
in such a synthesis. Christ is the instrument of God's saving
action on our behalf; how, therefore, is it possible that we
too should ourselves be sharers with God in this saving work?
This will be a really difficult question to answer if we

consider that God began his decisive work for us in the earthly life of Jesus, which, however, ended in disaster; and that the crucial steps in this work of redemption were taken when Christ underwent his atoning death on the Cross, suffered the agony of God-abandonment, descended into hell, and rose again on the third day. This last and most important sequence of events would seem to be impatient of any copying or imitation by us. For as long as we live, we ourselves can only perform finite acts against which the death and Resurrection of Christ, which clearly are not finite but eternal in character, stand out in sharp contrast.

Let us look first at the pattern of Christ's saving work. His earthly life runs a horizontal course from his Incarnation and his birth to the moment of his death. Then comes a sharp break, a drop: "He descended into Hell." He arrives in the realm where time and space are nonexistent, whereas

for us (on Holy Saturday), chronological or surface time continues. Then from the timeless, spaceless darkness of hell, the power and the glory of the Father resurrects him "on the third day" and raises him vertically to the horizontal plane he had left, lifting him whole and entire, body and soul into the eternal life of the Godhead. Such a pattern of life (if we may call it this) embraces a compass infinitely and incomprehensibly vaster than that normally reckoned to be the scope of an ordinary human existence. It spans the whole of time and extends beyond this into an eternity of two kinds. The first of these is the timelessness of the underworld, where all dimensions of time are lost and where all is reduced to a timeless "point of death"; and the second is what we may call "time which has no end", where the doors are flung open on to an expanse of eternity that stretches endlessly in every direction (a difficult notion indeed to describe adequately).

Now according to St. Paul, the whole of this extended pattern of life is to be taken as the measure of our life as Christians here on earth. If, according to him, we have already died with the dying Christ—sacramentally in baptism and existentially through our being crucified with Christ (see Gal 6:14)—but at the same time have been raised with him and given a place in heaven with him, in Christ Jesus (see Eph 2:6), we therefore live within a horizon and from sources that lie beyond the limits of our mortality. How, therefore, is this to be possible? How does God's involvement in Christ impinge upon our involvement as Christians? Is this divine/human encounter so wholly beyond our scrutiny that we can only argue that somehow, though in our mortal condition sinful and fallen, we are at the same time justified by God through Christ, which we may find difficult to appreciate but which we nonetheless accept in faith? Or is there a point where the divine intersects with the human, perceptible to our conscious minds, that we can realize as Christians?

Under the Old Covenant, we saw that Israel's response to God when he first called her by his grace was a response of total compliancy to the will of God and a corresponding willingness to be led into freedom by him. At least ideally this ought to have been so, for Israel never really succeeded in living up to her calling. Under the New Covenant, it is in the attitude of the Word-Made-Man, Jesus of Nazareth, that we can perceive the full realization of this total and unconditional willingness to submit to the guidance of the

Father's will. For only when in all seriousness a man declares *in advance* his willingness to agree to every divine decree, even should the decree be hidden and incalculable, can it be said that, in making this kind of response, his will is in perfect harmony with the will of God. The gift of God's grace alone, of course, makes this possible; but no violence is done to human nature in making such an act of submission. When a man says Yes to God, it is possible that God has destined him to suffering, darkness, and dereliction, a prospect sufficient to strike terror into the hearts of finite and mortal beings, and to cause them to draw back in fright because this is far more than the ordinary man can demand of himself, even when stretched to the limit. Hence there arises a conflict (like that on the Mount of Olives) between "my will" and "thy will"; yet it is the pact with God, made at the beginning, that finally triumphs over the promptings of his own will, because in the last resort his deepest inclination is to say Yes to the will of God. Only thus can a proper balance be achieved between the divine commandment and human consent. For under these circumstances, this allowing God to have his way is by no means the same as resigning oneself to fate or to the dominion of some superior being; it is rather a childlike surrender in trust of all that we have or are to the love of God, which we may indeed no longer feel, but which still, nonetheless, attracts our love in return. This is consent in its purest form as we find it in the New Testament. It is, after all, the action on which the whole of Jesus' existence is founded, who as God and man brought this aspect of unceasing self-surrender from the sphere of the divine into the midst of human existence. It is similarly the action fundamental to the life of his Mother, Mary, who signifies by her *Ecce ancilla* that she too has totally and unconditionally surrendered to the divine will; for she is purely womb, purely Matrix and Materia and Mater from which God may fashion whatever he will. She is thus a figure of the Church that, unlike the Synagogue of old, does not hang back reluctantly while her leader goes forward obediently, but corresponds in all things to her Head. In Mary heaven and earth finally converge, here the finite encounters the infinite. Heaven, being masculine, takes the initiative and bestows its infinity on the earth; the earth, endowed with the quality of infinity, responds accordingly and brings forth her fruit. In the same spirit Mary (and in her, the holy Church), without knowing what would happen, accompanied her Son through all the foreordained events of his life, through the God-abandonment on the Cross, through the darkness of death to the Resurrection. Thus we can see that the whole of God's action in Jesus Christ by grace can become the model for our involvement with God: in the work of liberating the world.

We now also understand why Jesus promised his disciples that they would "accomplish greater works" than he had done on earth. For the things he accomplished during his earthly ministry were but parables of his coming Passion and Resurrection. For example, he healed the sick, changed few loaves into many, walked on the water; and these are all stages on the way toward a reality that he describes as finishing his course (see Lk 13:32). Christians, however, through participating in his perfection now accomplished, derive from this the power to be effective in the world, aided as they are by the Holy Spirit, who himself proceeds from the perfected work of God.

This affords us another important insight. God acted in Christ, painstakingly and tirelessly for the sake of the poor, the sick, the stranger, the hungry, and the naked, for all those in fact imprisoned in the "Egyptian bondage" of this world of alienation, until eventually he took upon himself all our fallenness in the person of his Son. For Jesus expressly identified himself with all the poor of this world (see Mt 25:35ff.), in order that the Father might be able to recognize them all in him and therefore see him in all of them. If, however, we are to see the involvement of men as being harnessed at source with the divine involvement, then to be a Christian cannot simply mean to attempt to imitate God's involvement in our ethical, social, and political involvements by equally declaring our solidarity with the poor, the oppressed, the captive, and those who endure torture. Rather the significant factor in being a Christian is that he does all with reference to and in dependence on the ultimate source of his actions, through loving first and above all things, the God who loves us in Christ in order that he may then, by means of and together with love, turn his attention to the needs of those who are the object of the love of God. Only if we start from this "Alpha" will our involvement lead us to the "Omega" of the man who is loved, only thus will we succeed in caring for him inwardly in order that he may find his true destiny, only thus will we achieve that solidarity with him which is only possible in God. In the process of all this, however, we encounter the primary object of the love of God, namely, Jesus Christ, the God-man, who is at once the fullest expression of the divine activity as he is its consummation and who, being the focus of divine and human love, can never be disregarded nor bypassed. He is no mere transitory intermediary who will eventually be no longer required; he is in his role as mediator the everlasting midpoint in whom the love of God for us shines brightly and in whom our love for God and for our neighbor is gathered together into a unit. We can understand therefore why Paul, after the long labor of dictating the first letter to the Corinthians, finally takes the pen in his own hand to sign it and adds a last sentence (which presumably comes from a liturgy with which the Corinthians were familiar). "If any one has no love for the Lord [Jesus]," he writes, "let him be accursed" (1 Cor 16:22). Because if he does not love the Lord, he does not belong to the Christian community; he has no part in the table of the Lord, where Christ gives himself in love; he has not even understood the very heart of the Christian faith. Similarly, the Jesus of the Johannine writings demands that we love him, since the whole essence of the faith is simply that we should understand that the love that characterizes the life of the Trinity has been manifested in him, and in him has been abundantly proved (see Jn 8:42; 14:15, 21, 23–24, 28; 15:21, 23–24; 16:27; 21:15ff.; 1 Jn 2:15; 4:20; 5:1ff.). To say that love is the communion of Christians is not simply to enunciate an abstract principle; rather in the Christian communion of love we share in a personal act of God himself, the tip of which may be seen shining in the person of Christ, but which in its depths contains the interpersonal life of the Blessed Trinity and in its breadth embraces the love of God for the whole world.

3

SOME CONCLUSIONS

Tidings of Joy: Abiding in the Source

The joyful message of the gospel, the *eu-angelion*, is not primarily about faith or knowledge; still less is its primary purpose to provide us with a program for action. The gospel tells us of the receiving of great joy, joy greater than the heart of man can be persuaded of ("And while they still disbelieved for joy, and wondered"—Lk 24:41), for God is greater than our hearts (see 1 Jn 3:20), and the peace that he restores to us, having passed through death and hell (see Jn 20:19–21), "passes all understanding" (Phil 4:7). There is joy from the very beginning since, in the birth of the Messiah, all God's promises of old have been fulfilled and shown to be God's great Yes to the world (see 2 Cor 1:20); and since equally that most ancient of hopes with which our story began, namely, the hope that death one day would be vanquished, will come true in the destiny of Jesus. Then follows, however, the steep and rugged pathway, its difficulties increasing at every step, through the life of Jesus, along which we follow Jesus' tremendous efforts and the efforts of the disciples who followed him, often wondering, often not really understanding, to bring about God's involvement in the world. The preaching of salvation is no easy message; hard words are spoken, they are burning, and they allow no compromise, for the living word of God is like a hammer that breaks rocks in pieces (see Jer 23:29); like a sword dividing bone and marrow till all lies exposed before the judgment of God (Heb 4:12ff.); in every word, in every action of Jesus one feels God's involvement; we feel God striving; we sense the seriousness of his endeavor. Nothing in the life of Jesus is separate from God's involvement, nothing in his being beyond or above the embrace of the Father's action, for he is the Father's action, he it is, who constantly takes over and acts for and with the Father, guided step by step by the Holy Spirit. He spares himself little, and therefore his disciples and those who listen to him can expect to be spared no less.

Not that he thereby breaks or hurries the regular rhythm of normal human everyday existence, nor does he in any sense abuse it. Like any normal human being, he eats and sleeps, enjoys a feast, and goes to dinners. He knows times of happiness as he knows moments of anger, weeping, and weariness; he has times, too, for refreshment in prayer, in which one strengthens oneself afresh for involvement. But everything that the daily round of human existence prescribes for him is an instruction, everything is conditioned by his consent to that which will be seen for ever and ever (see Jn 5:19–20). For his whole life is characterized by his continually consenting to whatever the Father gradually reveals, since the whole of his existence as such is conditioned by the act of consent he made at the beginning to obey in all things the will of the Father (see Phil 2:6ff.). Thus for Jesus also, every effort he makes, every action he undertakes is based on an enduring agreement between him and the Father. This, like a pedal note, sounding beneath all the intricacies of the fugue of his actions controls and steadies the rhythm of the whole movement. But when at the Father's bidding, the long expected "hour" eventually comes, and Jesus rises from table and goes out into the darkness (see Jn 14:31), then that steadying pedal note seems to die away. The source of life from the Father is sealed off; the Father's presence is withdrawn, his light extinguished—and the Son, bearing the sin of the world, is abandoned by the Father (see Mk 15:34). Yet this state of abandonment, throughout which the Son does not cease to cry out to the Father, despite the Father's being concealed, is rather like a sculptor's mold or a photographic negative in its relation to the positive reality of a presence and a union that can never be disturbed. Only those as inseparably close to one another as Father and Son can experience this kind of abandonment. The Son understands this in the midst of a state of not understanding, when he says, "The hour is coming, indeed it has come, when you ... will leave me alone; yet I am not alone because the Father is with me" (Jn 16:32). This saying does not permit our concluding that in God's supreme involvement for the salvation of the world, when the Son is abandoned by the Father and the Father is himself "abandoned" by the Son, the "eternal blessedness" enjoyed by the Trinity in union somehow survives in the uppermost regions of the soul of the Son of Man. It is, after all, God who acts, and he involves himself to the very limit. Neither words nor concepts can be found to express God's allowing himself to be involved in the winds of destiny and storms of aggression that sweep through the world; but neither of these forces succeeds in entangling him or his power in the relentless destiny of the world. God instills his love with his power when he acts and suffers in the context of the freedom of the man, Christ Jesus. And this love goes its way into dereliction without being forced by anybody, not even by man's state of being lost. And because God can achieve this *by himself*, he has therefore been able to risk the creation of a world of free created beings and a world that knows aggression. That God's love is more resourceful than the cunning wickedness of men does not mean that the Creator has an unfair advantage in his ascendancy over the creature; for love does not conquer in the way that power conquers, but wins its victories precisely because it does not resort to power.

Victory, however, it is, and a real victory. The joy of Easter after all is founded on Christ's dereliction on the Cross and his abandonment in hell. For his abandonment was like the final testing of the unity of the Trinity, which as such is the fullness of joy. Not that the joy of the Divine Persons is an idle, self-indulgent kind of joy that they share in while the creature suffers; their joy penetrates deep into all the world's suffering; they share the experience of its misery, but their joy proves deeper than all sense of abandonment. For God's action on behalf of lost humanity is so final that every reproach levelled against the providential ordering of the world is put to silence. In the New Testament we read that joy is able to permeate not only the extremes of suffering and situations like the abandonment of God by God, but that it is also to be found in the face of the hardest demands, the most remorseless rebuke, even that most tragic of all divisions (between Jews and Christians, who stand divided before the Cross). Indeed the gospel would not have so evidently been a message of pure joy, had it not had power and courage to overcome the "great sorrow and unceasing anguish in my heart" (Rom 9:2); for the mighty promise of the love of God "comforts us in all our affliction" (2 Cor 1:4).

If man in faith receives this message of joy, he finds himself
in a strange predicament. On the one hand he learns that
God's greater love has overcome the world (see Jn 16:33),
and that even the last enemy, death, has had its sting withdrawn (see 1 Cor 15:55). He learns too that God acts first
before man can do anything, be anything or make any
response; and that when God acts, all is restored once more
to its true proportions. So too is he, who as man is the
beneficiary of God's gracious action. He can therefore make
no more suitable response than to surrender himself in childlike trust to this Source in whom all truth reposes. He determines once and for all to know no other "except Jesus Christ
and him crucified" and abandoned by God (1 Cor 2:2), lest
the Cross of Christ, the source of all power, should "be
emptied of its power" (1 Cor 1:17). Were he to resort to
relying on his own efforts and to turn his back on the pure
unmerited gifts that flow from this source, then "the stum-
bling block of the cross has been removed" (Gal 5:11).

On the other hand, however, this source cannot simply
be treated as if it were an established fact to be relied on,
nor regarded as an abstract truth to be pondered or a work
of art to be admired, nor dismissed with only a word of
thanks. For the source is not a thing, nor an abstract truth
nor a work of art, but God himself, eternally involved in
Christ crucified for my sake and for the sake of the whole
world. I myself cannot, in the face of this, stand by as a
mere spectator. I am involved, though involved only insofar as I involve myself. To put this less concisely, in the
process of God's involving himself for my sake, I am already
affected by his involvement. But it is not just the result of
God's efforts that benefits me; for through becoming
involved, I have inevitably entered into partnership with
that eternal love which is manifested as such in all the

tremendous work that love does in the world. Hence what we call the gift to the world of the free, unmerited grace of God is in fact his involvement on behalf of the world, in which, however, the world itself is already and eternally involved.

In a strange way, this removes the dualism between prayer and works, between contemplation and action. One normally imagines that for a Christian (as for every person who has some religion), action is the fruit of contemplation though contemplation can and must continue throughout the action and fertilize it. This much is not untrue; for in Christianity, as in every religion, God as the Absolute enjoys the primacy that is due to him, and we must therefore, first of all, turn to him in order that we may know him and be able to proclaim him to others. All our actions in the world should echo and correspond to this initial experience of God; for the grace of God is prior to all our involvement, undertaken for God in the world, and for the needs of the world for his sake. But this golden rule, to which there is no exception, is substantially modified in Christianity by the fact that the source of grace at which I as an individual must first of all drink is nothing less than God's total involvement, everything he does in fact for the salvation of the world. Were I not involved in this saving action of his, I would never learn that God is love, the love of three Persons in One. For I can never strip away the whole dramatic action of the Incarnation, Cross, and Resurrection in the attempt to contemplate "behind all this" God as he fundamentally "is", everlastingly at rest, and content in himself. What we are looking at when we contemplate the love of God is "Christ, giving himself in love" and this "urges us on, because we are convinced that one has died for all; therefore all have died" (2 Cor 5:14). In contemplating this, we suddenly realize that we have been made to take our part in the action as a whole and that we are therefore participants in this action. God's active work "urges us on" to active works. For since he has laid down his life for us, we too ought to lay down our lives for the brethren (see 1 Jn 3:16). In the act of contemplation, we are at once drawn deeper into the springing source and at the same time thrust out from the source into our own channels of activity. If, however, we go about our active work in the *right* way, we shall paradoxically find ourselves penetrating yet deeper into the source. For the freedom we are looking for is in the last resort already given to us in the source.

We can neither simplify nor abandon this argument, and we must in particular warn severely against any attempt at simplification. Under no circumstances may we turn our backs on the source of God's grace, treating it like a piece of knowledge we learned in the past, but with which by now we are all too familiar, or like a valuable object that long ago came into our possession and of which we are now able to make practical use by exchanging for ready money. For the source is God's mouth, and we must never take our mouths away from it. So, too, the source is the ever-present Christ event through which we are channelled into the way of being our true selves and are enabled to remain in the way of truth. The Johannine writings talk of "staying", for the idea is basic to their thought. "They came", the Fourth Gospel says, "and saw where he was staying and they *stayed* with him that day" (Jn 1:39). On the other hand, "They went out from us, but they were not of us; for if they had been of us, they would have continued [stayed] with us" (1 Jn 2:19). For to stay in this sense means simply "to go on receiving one's true self at the hand of the gracious action of God, being at the same time overwhelmed with thankfulness, and brought to our knees in homage before the wonder of unconditional love". This is what St. Paul has in mind when he talks of "praying without ceasing" (see 1 Thess 1:2; 2:13; 5:17; 2 Thess 1:3, 11; 2:13; Rom 1:10; 1 Cor 1:4; Eph 5:20; Phil 1:4; Col 1:3; Philem 4; cf. Lk 18:1); and Origen provides a delightfully human explanation of how such prayer is in fact possible.

> To pray without ceasing, [he writes (*de orat.* 12.2)] is to join one's prayer with one's daily work and to unite suitable actions to one's prayer; for even good works or the fulfilling of God's commandments are to be included as a part of prayer. We can only accept the command to "pray without ceasing" as practicable if we conceive of the whole life of the believer as one great unbroken prayer; of which great prayer, what we are accustomed to call prayer is a part.

The source contains riches sufficient to bless all our activities in this world with fruitfulness, if—and only if—we keep ourselves alive by abiding in the source and never wander away. For here alone is true fruitfulness, and the more we permit this spring of life to touch and quicken the springs of our existence, the more we allow this, the supreme Action, to be the principle of all our actions, the more, too, we shall be rich in fruit. So, too, the more like young children we are in opening our hearts to this source to receive its riches, the more grown-up and adult we shall be in opening our hearts to give to the world and its needs.

For the Christian there are many dimensions to this act of "abiding in the source". It is understandably an act of a very personal nature that we perform consciously and involves us in being open, ready to listen to and obey God's word, and in being prepared to give time to contemplation in order to allow the rain from heaven to soak its way in. For only when we have received the word of God can we rightly return it in the words of prayer from the depths of our own hearts. In our personal relationship to God, however, we are never private individuals, and therefore our openness to God has always, just as directly, a social dimension, experienced when together we listen to the word of God as preached by the Church, when we take part together in the Eucharist, when we discuss the word of God with our brothers and sisters in the faith. To bring about the community life of the Church, to make the community real and its sharing effective, is no secondary consideration, but a direct way of abiding in the source and of realizing the presence of the source in every aspect of our existence. For Catholics, Christ and the Church, which came into being through him, are together simultaneously both fountain and source of grace. But as Mary existed before her child, yet was only enabled to become his mother through the involvement of the child, so too in the life of the individual Christian, the Church may exist before he does. Yet the Church teaches him what he knows full well: that she is only a source insofar as she owes her existence to the joint involvement of Christ and the Father.

It is the practice of Christian living to learn more and more never to desert the source, even in the midst of our secular activity. We can learn this only if we consciously put it into practice, which means our constantly going back from our worldly distractions to reflecting on the source. Gradually, without any unnatural training, an integrating process takes place in our psychological constitution. For the source continues to flow through us, even when we are absorbed in our daily affairs. And we should add here that we are dutybound to devote ourselves wholeheartedly and with undivided attention to these occupations. The fact that despite all this, we still abide in the source, or rather the source never ceases to flow in us, is because God, in his involvement for the world, has made us members of himself and instruments of his action.

Hence we now realize in our own existence what in the source Christ has realized eucharistically with his Church. For Christ, the Eucharist means two things simultaneously. On the one hand, it means surrendering himself so totally into the hands of the Father, that the Father is therefore able to give him in return as bread broken and wine outpoured for the life of the world. But it means equally his entering so wholeheartedly into his active service of the world, that he becomes effective in the lives of others not only by what he says and what he does, but somehow his entire person is the vehicle of his influence.

Considering our Neighbor

The transition from the Church to the world is fluid. If we who constitute the living community of the Church share a common life in the source, then we are striving to allow to be operative in our own community the kind of divine society that Jesus Christ has opened up for the world as a whole. Now, in order to create a church community as Christ would wish it to be, we must learn from the very beginning not to use our natural eyes when looking at our neighbor, nor the categories of everyday psychology as the measure of his worth. Rather must we look at him "with the eyes of faith" so that we may see him as God sees him in Jesus Christ. Many passages in the Pauline Epistles, which are all more or less concerned with this question, warn us of the importance and at the same time the difficulty of seeing people in this way. To all appearances, there is still a difference between husband and wife, master and servant, Jew and Gentile, strong and weak, wise and foolish, but in the eyes of God, these are not different but on a level, and this is how the Christian must see them. Furthermore, where these distinctions express a difference in degree, our normal assessment of the values expressed in these differences is completely reversed;

> but God chose what is foolish in the world to shame the wise,
> God chose what is weak in the world to shame the strong,
> God chose what is low and despised in the world, even things
> that are not, to bring to nothing things that are (1 Cor 1:27–28).

On the other hand, however, there can be no question of the weak and foolish raising itself up to a position whence it is able to look down on the strong and the wise (for if this were so, Nietzsche's complaint would be fully justified); but each of these, as poles in a dialectical process understandable only in the light of Christianity, should relate as members of the one body to their one Lord who is their common head. For it is not the conclusions that may be drawn as to his natural abilities that will determine our neighbor's function in the Body of Christ, but rather his place in the Body will be decided by the task allotted to him by the Head (see Eph 4:11; cf. Rom 12:3); and this function gives him a special place in the Church for the benefit of all the other members. The corollary to this is that when a Christian is given a task to fulfill or called to a particular vocation, the task he is called to coincides exactly with his Christian character. Inside the Church, which is basically a network of people possessing different charisms, the pattern of human relationships matches exactly the pattern according to which the various charismatic functions are interwoven. This means, therefore, that I must now unreservedly learn to see my fellow Christians in the light of the task that Christ has determined that they should fulfill. For the grace of Christ and his mission for them has made them into what they are in the eyes of God, and into what they are to be for me.

Clearly, not all Christians have reached a state of perfect holiness, and therefore not every Christian fully lives up to his calling. Because this is so, we have, on the one hand, the Church in her teaching office warning us that we must bear with one another in patience, never forgetting that we give others much to endure (see Phil 2:3ff.; Gal 6:2; Eph 4:2); and, on the other hand, it is freely given to us to exercise the office of correcting one another "in a spirit of gentleness" (Gal 6:1).

The community life of the Church, however, is in itself only the visible model of what the community life of all people ought to be, since it is the whole world that has been liberated by Christ. The believer therefore cannot regard any non-Christian neighbor differently from the way in which he regards his fellow Christian. For the former, too, is what he is in the light of heavenly truth, insofar as he is beloved of God and has been set free by the Son; and God has involved himself for him no less absolutely than he has for me and for the Church's faithful. So long as we abide in the source and allow God's original involvement to become effective in us, our involvement on behalf of the stranger whom we do not know, whoever he may be (as in the parable of the good Samaritan), can be no less than our involvement on behalf of those of our own household. For in that all those for whom Christ died are his brothers and sisters, the Church's communion already stands open to the whole world, not of course in a vague humanitarian or cosmopolitan sense, but simply because the Christian, being a conscious and responsible believer, always involves himself for others according to the scheme of the divine involvement.

Clearly we cannot practically spend ourselves to the limit for all men. The finiteness of our powers and the ordinary limitations of our existence impose a certain order on the way in which we give of ourselves. There is a hierarchy of values. St. Thomas Aquinas in the *Summa Theologica* sought to establish an objective order; but valid as his rules may be, everyday life opposes them again and again with other unforeseeable rules of its own. We meet the man who fell among thieves on his journey, and all our plans for the person we were going to see have to be changed, because this man is now the immediate object of our concern. For Christianity has shed the light of love over humanity and in this light the unique worth of every individual person is made manifest. Without this light the general principles of human rights could not have been formulated, principles that are normative indeed for us, even though in practice they are frequently trodden underfoot. But the darkness falls on Christianity deepest of all when ostensibly Christian nations pay no heed to these principles, whereas others that do not call themselves Christian seek to conform themselves on the whole to such principles. In vain we shall search the world before Christ for this kind of outlook of man on his fellow man; we shall find it neither in Plato, who speaks nobly of Eros, nor in the treatises of Aristotle and Cicero on friendship nor even in the writings of the Stoics. In none of these will we find the kind of respect for the person of one's neighbor that can only be established as a principle for the first time by the Christian revelation. For God, in his boundless involvement, has indeed always the individual in mind (though all in community are just as much his preoccupation); and as he moves toward the individual, so he lights up his unique dignity as a person. But should the source of God's gracious involvement fall into oblivion, then sooner or later the face of the person will become indistinct, and he will sink back once more into mere anonymity.

Because, however, the most significant thing in life that can happen to our neighbor is his being laid claim to and taken seriously as a person, an event that leaves on him the most lasting impression, a state that constitutes for him the source of the greatest happiness he can know on earth, in this above all lies the credibility of the Church, and the success of the mission of Christianity.

It ought therefore to be possible to recognize the Christian by the fact that he opens the very depths of his heart to his brother and shows him its inmost recesses, thereby demonstrating to him that his heart, too, has already had its secret places plundered and indwelt, that there is communion between these depths of being—in him alone, however, who has endured their common closing of their hearts against him, and who has granted to both the gift of divine communion. The Christian ought next to proceed from this living proof of the reality of the Holy Trinity to a theoretical demonstration of its truth. And the pain and self-denial that it costs him to disarm himself so fully before his fellow man in order that he may bear him past turning away and closing his heart against him ought then to lead him to point his brother to the Man on the Cross. Again, from that communion which develops when human hearts unite, his brother ought to have some intimation of what the Church truly is. And this always because the Christian draws all his strength from the source that is freely given him and never for one moment presents himself as equal with or as a substitute for this source, neither for God, nor for Christ, nor for the Church.

Here now we have, too, the answer to the first problem we raised in the Introduction. We asked how the Church in transcending the world could have anything left for her interior life save the lifeless machinery of its institutional form. For if the Church is as Christ envisaged her and as the apostles attempted to build her, this danger is indeed avoided. For the interior life of the Church is then one of selfless love so fully exercised that, within its communion, the structure of its ministries coincides exactly with that of interpersonal relationships and the whole is the visible manifestation of a community that so gives of itself unselfishly in love and service that it cannot fail to touch the world outside, both as a community as through its individual members who perhaps spend their lives principally among non-Christians as "children of God without blemish in the midst of a crooked and perverse generation, among whom you shine as lights in the world" (Phil 2:15). The apparent surplus of ministerial office, which arouses so much opposition in the world outside and makes the Church lacking in credibility, is in the actual plan simply the means of guaranteeing the selflessness of love and of drawing all the manifold involvements of Christians back together to the one eucharistic involvement of Christ, from which all the Church's life proceeds and in which she remains.

The Christian Hope

What hope and expectation fills the Church and the Christian as they move beyond the confines of their own existence out into the world of non-Christian humanity? This cannot be expressed by a single concept. The dimensions of Christian hope, measured against those of what is called world history, seem at once both greater and yet smaller than the latter. Let us cast our minds back for a moment to that broken diagram of the saving event that bears the name of Jesus Christ. Christ's life pursues a horizontal course up to his death; then comes a drop and, descending into hell, Christ enters into solidarity with all those who have died in body and in spirit. Then vertically, he is lifted from the "underworld" up into the "world above" of God's eternity. This is the great pattern to which the Church and every Christian's life must be wholly subordinate; and that pattern at its center shows us pointedly that the power of death has indeed been broken and its forces overcome. St. Paul maintains that this breaking of the power of death constituted from the very beginning the ultimate meaning of Israel's faith (see Rom 4:17–25; cf. 1 Cor 15:4). Now, however, mortality is the inescapable condition of man's life in secular history. The subject of secular history, however, is not an abstract humanity that exists unassailed throughout the centuries, but rather the concrete number of human beings, thousands of whom die at every moment. History is concretely put together from an infinite number of finite moments; and the deathless continuity we create by the exclusion of all real deaths is indeed a secondary phenomenon of time. What we call the advance of humanity, be this cultural, technical, or, as some would maintain, moral, can at best be related to this secondary or artificial kind of time, from which dying, which is a phenomenon of time in its primary sense, has been excluded. In this respect, even the hope that in the perspective of world history, the world in years to come will be a "better world" than it was in the past or even in the present, is from the Christian point of view at best a secondary kind of hoping. For Christian hope is characterized by the involvement of Jesus Christ, by his resurrection victory over death. Even were one in one's more idealistic or foolish moments to hold out hopes that in the years ahead one day a victory might be gained over man's mortality, still by this nothing whatever would have been achieved for the entirety of times past or present. Christian hope, however, is related substantially to men of every generation—past, present, and future; St. Paul tells us expressly that the last generation before Christ's Second Coming, of whom it may not be required that they should die, will in no way "precede those who have fallen asleep" (1 Thess 4:15). For the real object of the Christian's hope is to overcome the boundaries of death that cross the stream of human history at every moment, as to all appearances it flows onward on its course.

If we reflect on this quite soberly, we shall realize that God's involvement in world history on behalf of all men destined to death affords no ("theological") hopes for the historical future. If it did, then God would no doubt be even now intervening in his creation and setting it to rights. This would not be worthy of him. For when he set men on the earth that they might increase and subdue the earth (see Gen 1:28), when he "clothed him in strength, like his own" (Sir 17:2), but directed them to "seek God, in the hope that they might feel after him and find him" (Acts 17:27), he endowed them from the beginning with freedom and responsibility. They were to enter on the future that opened up before them with this manifold commission to accomplish, and inherent in this charge given in their creation (and written into the very being of man himself) is the hope that it is patient of fulfillment so long, that is to say, as man remains true to his own nature as it was created and endeavors to develop it in freedom and lives responsibly in accordance with it. All this, of course, has been deeply affected by our social, personal, and indeed cosmic fallenness; and those laws, written into nature herself, the will to power, the principle of aggression, and the submersion of the noblest in life by the common and vulgar, constantly make all human striving seem ambiguous and in the end to be vain (see Rom 8:19). And yet, this sense of futility does not release man from his responsibility in shaping and building up the world of nature and the world of humanity; and it is in this responsibility that is contained a hope that carries him forward against the running tide of futility.

Now we must emphasize that this form of hope, insofar as it is directed toward some earthly prospect, is not replaced by Christian hope, because the latter has a different objective, namely, the salvation of the whole world, and of the whole of history, past, present, and future, seeing it lifted into the eternal life of God himself, an objective that stands at right angles to all possible objectives and circumstances that lie in the path of secular time. But it is precisely because there is a difference between secular and Christian hope that the latter can have a decisive significance for the world. Secular hope has been truly broken; every moment it is concretely shattered at death. Beyond my death, there is no hope for me in the secular future. Is there any for others? But then again every other individual has each his own death in front of him. But how, if death is now no longer able to destroy hope because its sting has been withdrawn? The power of death, however, has already been fundamentally broken by death itself being included in the infinite consent and willingness of Jesus to obey in all things his Father's loving will, when death itself became the most radical expression of the loving purposes of the Father. And the power of death is yet more radically broken by Jesus in his death taking upon himself the whole world's guilt, suffering it in the state of God-abandonment, whereby the ground for man's despair, hopelessness, and resignation to fate is wholly cut away.

For this reason, the Christian can pursue his course through the world with fresh hope, furnished from its source in the divine. Insofar as he himself abides by this source and quenches his own thirst here, he too can open up the way to this source to others who likewise thirst, can even through his own person give to others to drink out of this same source (see Jn 4:14; 7:3ff.). Around him he can create a model of existence that is both personally and socially freed from the powers of the world and provides a foretaste of the risen life way beyond death in all its possible forms, an existence that is indeed to some extent hidden (see Col 3:3) yet possessed of such effectiveness that it exercises a powerful influence over the whole complex of human society. Indirectly and indeed very indirectly, the outer structures of this society can be touched by the inner change; and quite indirectly it can be concluded from such a change in the structures that there is an agent of change in the society. But here we come against an insuperable barrier. "[T]he form [schēma] of this world is passing away" (1 Cor 7:31). A changed structure is no guarantee of a change in spirit, even if the changing spirit was the cause of the change in the structure.

It remains a significant sign that Christian involvement in its most thoroughgoing forms has always been initiated with a persistent and sometimes almost stubborn preference for places where, humanly speaking and from the point of view of this world, no further hope remains or where no involvement seems worth the trouble. Christians care for the dying, for life grown old and worn out, for the incurably sick, for the mentally ill, or for the handicapped, amongst whom sometimes they can expect not so much as a smile by way of thanks. We should not ask whether such undertakings make sense or are worthwhile, for they were begun as a challenge to the meaninglessness of this world, in the full consciousness that, in an involvement of this sort, only Christian understanding of hope alone becomes apparent in a very pure form. Now the genius of Christianity both ought and could with this same quietly challenging kind of freedom move out into all the other structures of human society, which indeed have something of the hopelessness of the dying and the sick and those with mental illness about them; and the Christian might go about caring for and dealing with society, bringing that same hope which persists beyond the boundaries of death, yet which nevertheless takes death into account. It will be objected that such a program of action demands the character of a saint. This may well be; but from the very beginning, Christian living has always been most credible, where at the very least it has shown a few faint signs of true holiness.

PART TWO

OUR INVOLVEMENT

4

INTRODUCTORY

Man in Relation to God

Our purpose in what now follows is to attempt to put our achievement so far on yet deeper foundations, in order to draw some more concrete conclusions.

The Christian's involvement has its origins in God's involvement for the sake of the world; it is grounded in it, captivated by it, shaped and directed by it. He turns, therefore, with God to the world. He now asks himself who it is that he meets in this world of which he himself, of course, is a part. He meets the man by whose wisdom and folly the wisdom and folly of all other things in the world is decided. An evolutionary portrait of the world provides a "scientific" foundation for this ancient Christian saying; and whoever allows that man has truly freedom to choose between the good and the evil will scarcely be able to keep on looking for a superman who at the most might be more powerful but in no way freer than man. The question still remains, however, what could this more powerful man begin to do with his power in his freedom? Hence we are firmly directed to the question concerning man; and the Christian faces this question whenever he asks himself for whom it is that he by God's grace is to involve himself.

Where does man become complete in himself? Where does he cease because of his freedom to be an open question mark? Before we start, we may exclude any solution that reckons the free individual man to be but a means toward the planning of the future of mankind. That an individual may also place his life in the service of a "better future" (and indeed must, after what we have just said) is self-evident. But were he compelled to surrender his freedom entirely to such plans, then his very nature would be both destroyed and denied.

One free agent is constantly searching for another. And the best thing that can happen to a man in his finite condition to make him happy is to be recognized for his true worth by a free person who accepts him freely on terms of intimacy. Part of the meaning of human existence is satisfied when people meet and live together in such a relationship. But what about the whole meaning? For the more irrevocably two people love one another in freedom, the more tragic then appears their mortality. It may well be of some consolation that after the death of the beloved, be this spouse or child or friend, the wound is healed albeit gradually by the laws of nature, and that there follows a guilt-free kind of unfaithfulness; this may well help to support the human species. But such gentle cynicism calls in question all that is most valuable and unique in human freedom of choice and thrusts man down once more into the domain of "nature". The contradiction between a surrender, irrevocable as it is intentional, and death (or quite simply, the "law of transformation") remains insoluble; and man in his finite existence *is* this contradiction.

Ancient religious cultures including Christianity have seen all this quite plainly and have therefore related man to a supernatural and divine sphere of existence. Let us, however, confine ourselves to the Christian view on this matter. St. Thomas Aquinas, who combines the wisdom of the past—and of St. Augustine in particular—with the insights of the future, including those of modern times, affords us some enlightenment as to the paradox of man's transcendence. After having shown that there are not many ways in which man's freedom is able to find complete fulfillment, and having discoursed on particular goods that in every case fail to bring fulfillment—on riches, honors, and fame (or posthumous reputation); on power (!), health of body, sensual pleasure (coarse or sophisticated), and inner quiet of soul—he then shows that only the eternal God can fulfill the longing gaze of human freedom (see ST I, 2, q. 2). But if in the encounter between two people, neither power nor magic may be the instrument whereby free intimacy may be surreptitiously achieved but that this intimacy must disclose itself of its own accord, then how much the more we should expect the absolute and eternal Thou to invite man into a relationship with himself in perfect freedom and by grace that is wholly unmerited. Man of his own self has no "claim" he can make on God, not even though in the last resort he is unable to fulfill himself without God's free revealing of himself. In the light of some philosophies of our own day (notably philosophies of personal being that discuss "the life of dialogue") our conclusions concerning the paradoxical nature of man's inmost being are shown to be both necessary and fully justified. For if the free turning of one man to another cannot be brought about by compulsion, how much the less can we compel God's gracious self-disclosure of the most secret places of his heart. The highest dignity that man can know, which raises him above all the orders of nature, is to be ranked in virtue of his freedom with him who is freest of all. St. Thomas is fully aware that nature has furnished man (as she has all other natural beings) with the necessary resources and equipment to enable him to fulfill his immediate aims and purposes on this earth. He is also aware, however, that when the question of the ultimate meaning of his freedom arises, the laws of his natural being go into abeyance, and another principle takes over operation (which St. Thomas borrows, out of courtesy, from Aristotle): "Nobler [he writes] in his constitution is the being who is able to attain the supreme good even though he stands in need of assistance from outside to attain this end, than he who attains a lesser good by the aid of his own resources" (ibid., q. 5, a. 5). St. Thomas puts into practice the portrait of man supplied in Paul's speech on the Areopagus, where man is portrayed as subject to the finite limitations of time and space (God has determined for man "allotted periods" and "boundaries of their habitation") and yet represented as engaged in the single-minded pursuit of grasping and searching for the Absolute ("that they should seek God, in the hope that they might feel after him and find him"—Acts 17:27); throughout all of which God reserves himself the right to meet man in his searching and to satisfy his questing whenever and in whatever way he chooses.

In his book *Surnaturel* (1947; no E.T.), which was at first subject to some criticism but which in its expanded version (*Augustinisme et théologie moderne*, 1965; E.T., *Augustinianism and Modern Theology*, 1969, and *Le mystère du surnaturel*, 1965; E.T., *The Mystery of the Supernatural*, 1967) is quite beyond reproach, Henri de Lubac drew attention to the whole paradox of man as represented by the entire classical tradition. He does so by dismissing as both superfluous and unrealistic modern naturalistic models of man that give the impression that man might conceivably have been created by God in a state of "pure nature" and in this state have been able to attain by nature a final and satisfying end within this world; and further that God had only secondarily decided positively to orientate man toward a supernatural end within the Godhead for which he then provided him with the means of grace necessary to the achievement of this end. In this view, man is reduced to the level of a "natural being" who belongs essentially to this world, and his capacity for transcendence and entry into the sphere of the freedom and love of God is seen as a mere chance manifestation; God's whole involvement for the world in Christ's Incarnation, Cross, and Resurrection (in which, indeed, according to Ephesians 1:3–10 the Creator's original design for the world is revealed) is virtually represented as something superadded, to be dispensed with if necessary, and man is simply made more attentive to the satisfying of his needs and aims in this world.

De Lubac's radicalism, however, which in itself is but a modern exposition of the radicalism of all great Christian thinkers, is of considerable consequence for our whole concept of Christian involvement in the world. For only the Christian is in a position to judge clearly how basically unsatisfying it is for man, both as an individual and as a social being, to have as his ultimate goal the civilizing and humanizing of the world, because he himself has found his own fulfillment in the person of Jesus Christ. Some brilliant Christian thinkers of recent times, such as Maurice Blondel in his book *Action* (1893) and Emmanuel Mounier in some of his personal manifestoes (1934), have recognized this to be of fundamental importance. Teilhard de Chardin has taken this into account, too, when he refuses to allow that the story of the natural inner-historical evolution of mankind (as seen in history) leads automatically to the final transcendant Omega point and represents instead all man's cultural activity and his greatest efforts to civilize, socialize, and personalize the world as being but a *preparation d'un holocauste*, the building up of a great funeral pyre, into which from on high alone the lightning can descend out of pure grace, and entering it transform the whole, wrapping world and God together in a blaze of living union ("Deuxième Mémoire du P. Teilhard", in *Blondel et Teilhard de Chardin: correspondance commentée par H. de Lubac* [Paris: Beauchesne, 1965], p. 43; cf. p. 91). "The whole of our work [he writes] must ultimately be directed to forming the material for the sacrifice made ready to be kindled by the living flame from heaven." In this, Blondel and Teilhard are at one.

If it is true, however, that man is endowed *by his very nature* with the capacity to begin the work of making the earth his subject and of humanizing the world, and similarly true that his nature grants him power to step out beyond the limits of the natural order toward a goal that in his own strength he cannot attain, then only the Christian, and he alone, since he knows God's involvement for the world in Christ, will be able to direct aright man's strivings in this world and his efforts to attain transcendence. This does not mean that, by dint of sheer human superiority, he is in a position to offer his fellow men a "synthesis" of nature and supernature, like some design for freedom easy to handle. For this synthesis belongs uniquely to God himself; only he can perceive it; it is essentially eschatological in character and passes way beyond the limits of finite conception. For the risen Christ, who appears to his disciples in "a strange form", then at times allows himself to be recognized in a flash and afterward immediately withdraws, is certainly not a principle to be made use of and handled like some working hypothesis. He is at best the very highest end of all Christian and human hope, who keeps us alive and striving in the right direction, amid the fear that we might at the last have striven in vain. On the way toward this goal where the divine involvement and man's striving are finally to coincide, there is no clear pattern of development. And this because in the purposes of the Creator, only fragmentary plans have been made for man in his creatureliness. He is set within the teleological framework of this world, supplied with tasks whose purpose lies within the limits of this world, which altogether like man himself constitute but the preliminary to a goal, and man's inability to reach this goal by his own efforts, as St. Thomas says, is what finally constitutes his true nobility.

A Negative Proof

In the first section of this book, we took as our starting point the involvement of God. And we saw that in the world of the Bible, God, in moving out to meet us, stimulates in us the urge, deep-rooted in our being, to burst out beyond the bonds of earthly finitude toward him. In pagan religions, such longings after God have always something of a dreamlike quality and the images used to express them are clearly projections of the human imaginations. But man knows the problems inherent in his use of imagination; and he is therefore in mystical and negative theology fully prepared to see these dream images as having only relative significance, to inquire into what lies beneath them and ultimately to get rid of them altogether. For neither fantasy nor concept can express the true object of man's real longing. Nor can he know this of himself; for only God can reveal it to him.

In the world of the Bible, this is different. Here God is represented in the act of setting out in front of man on a journey into a future, unknown and yet assured. And man advances toward him, who himself is this unknown future. As God goes before man, as on the journey through the wilderness, he makes man live in a state of perpetual setting out toward that future which alone will bring him fulfillment. For there is no longer any question of man's psychosomatic unity being separated out into its constituent elements (as in pagan religions) by his agonizing longing for transcendence (here an immortal soul, there a discarded mortal body, neither of which is any longer "man"). It is a question rather of man being led by the God who goes before toward a genuinely human fulfillment—to a land "flowing with milk and honey". The prospect of this land he enters, however, fills him with disappointment. For new pictures of new lands and of this land transformed and altered are projected by the prophets for the future (most strongly by the Deutero- and Trito-Isaiah); and their vision is of an earthly Jerusalem, shining with the power and glory of God for all to see, which is to be the center of the world that will finally come. Once more the fulfillment of his hopes eludes him, and the images of the promises to come fade away into nothingness; or, to put this better: the eschatological pathos, alive in Israel from the beginning, became more and more accentuated so that the visions of the prophets lapsed into being but symbols of their transcending dynamic for the future, as Israel's real feeling for the eschatological emerged in late Jewish apocalyptic in its purest form. Here man's future, which hitherto had been thought of in terms of the horizontal prolongation of his history, is now seen clearly as breaking in from above into the old world, fallen and beyond redemption, which cannot transform itself from within, but needs recasting in her new and final shape by some power from on high.

In the Old Testament, then, a rift opens up more and more clearly that was at least latently present when God first made the promise, but which had widened to almost intolerable proportions by the time of late Judaism. One can see this in the writings of the Qumran community, which in the plans for the final battle at the end of the age, when the promised Kingdom of God will finally break in, depict a violent scene in which man's final efforts toward this end (in the carefully drawn-up plan of battle, which in its attention to detail foreshadow the plans that Marxism designs for its campaigns) converge with the mighty acts of God, who intervenes in this very battle with his two Messiahs, and brings about the final victory. Any idea, however, that the plans of men coincide exactly with the action prepared by God or rather that the divine involvement will draw all human striving into the sphere of its own operation belongs to the sphere of the Utopian and belongs to a dimension outside time (if one looks at this in the perspective of this-worldly history). For neither the place nor the time of God's inbreaking can be calculated in advance.

The dialectical processes of the Old Covenant go yet further. On the one hand, it becomes continually more clear that the sorrows of our mortal condition are closely associated with a state of subservience to the law (which in this sense means being the servants of an omnipotent God who imposes this law on man). Already in the Book of Job we find that such a situation leads to a fundamental kind of rebellion. Job appeals to a higher court of justice superior to either him or the Lord God, basically for the removal of the heteronomy that expresses itself as much in that kind of suffering that ends in death as in the imposition of the law.

In Judaism, as late as the works of Kafka, this kind of rebellion against a heteronomous guilt pronounced against a man from without and against an incomprehensible Lord who conceals himself recurs in many different forms. But is not perhaps this heteronomy presented together with the irremovable difference between man who is finite and creaturely and the God who is infinite and the Creator? The only alternative therefore (if we look at this from the perspectives of the Old Covenant) is to inquire behind the law (which after all, as St. Paul says, only came afterward; see Rom 5:20), and return to Abraham's Utopian faith in the resurrection of the dead (see Rom 4:17–25), for this first driving force of the Old Covenant was already pregnant with the final result, it is at work in the background of all prophetic activity (see Ezek 37; Is 26:19), and at the same time its final aim is the removal of the heteronomy we have been talking about, because God's law is to be instilled into human hearts so that men may obey it freely (see Jer 31:33; Ezek 11:19), and man will relate to God, not as a servant to his master but as a friend to his friend or as a child to his parents (see Jn 15:15; 8:35). Under the Old Covenant, however, such an outlook is altogether excessive; and when it is combined with those tendencies always latent in man to rebel against the Lord his God, the result in modern Judaism is man being represented as by origin an autonomous being who has given himself a heteronomous law (perhaps he had to do this, as Freud and the later Scheler suggest, in order to reach civilization), who, however, is able to see through the limitations he has imposed upon himself (cf. not only Freud but also Bergson and Simmel) and must loose his inhibitions (Marcuse) in order to reach the source of his inner drives and of his power. In this kind of Judaism, where the law is criticized out of existence as being something that merely "came afterwards", and in "negative thinking", freedom has the last and perhaps most puzzling word (Horkheimer, Adorno) and there the hopes of man and his history thrust them out into the sphere of the merely Utopian (Ernst Bloch), completely overturning all existing situations for the sake of the absolutely new, which exists only then. (Ludwig Rubiner: "*Dasein* itself does not exist, that which subsists does not exist, we ourselves are the first to make everything" [*Der Mensch in der Mitte*, 1920, p. 142.]) Alternatively one can, instead of pointing to the thinking without rules of primitive man (Lévy-Bruhl), manipulate the law system from the standpoint of one's own freedom (Wiener) or even equate law and nature as being primitively a structure without subject (Lévi-Strauss).

Such is the dialectic of Judaism (as Hegel saw it), the contradiction in human nature becoming seething and virulent through the coming of God, a nature that has been created for a purpose, and now realizes that it has been set in motion toward that end, which by its own powers it could not attain. The end toward which the whole world is orientated is that unity of divine and human freedom in Jesus Christ, which God alone can effect, for in Christ man finds his own self and is taken up whole and entire into God, in him the urge of Jewish messianic hopes is set at rest, provided that it is agreed to accept the synthesis as being God's grace, and not the goal that Israel is able to reach by dint of its own messianic power. For that driving force innate in the chosen people leads horizontally into the historical future, but it also leads to the transcendence of this horizontal line. Israel, however, cannot herself resolve this difference, for it is the hollow space in which the figure of the God-man is to be inscribed, who has fulfilled the destiny of all men, even to death and the hopelessness of hell, and transcends this destiny by his resurrection from the dead. For this reason, Jewish ideology in its *brisance* as

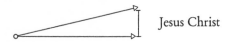 Jesus Christ

in its dialectic remains the enduring negative proof for the necessity of the Christ event. Jewish thought presses for a change in the structure of the world and of society, because their present structures are so closely allied in principle with the laws of aggression and death. It is always, however, only the structures of *this* world and *this* society that Judaism feels must be changed, because the messianic promise is directed toward a temporal future. Should Judaism succeed in changing the structures from the roots upward and lifting the law imposed from above from its hinges, then by this it would in fact bring about a change of heart. The heteronomy of servitude would lie behind us; we would have passed into a realm of freedom, a world of the positively human (Marx). It is impossible, however, to imagine such a step being taken; it belongs to the sphere of the Utopian, because it implies the removal of that which is to be changed. Judaism, above all religions, ought to have known how to wait in expectation for God to act. But instead of having the faith to wait for God, she took the management of the messianic kingdom into her own hands and either transformed the meaning of the law promulgated by God as the way to freedom, so that it became a "work" involving the taxing and burdensome labors of man's own resources (whereas, in fact, it is only by love in its fullness, as St. Paul shows, that the law can truly be fulfilled), or else in the light of the prophecies of Utopia, she has totally excluded all God's part from the law and, taking prophecy into her own hands, has made it into an enormous human achievement.

We can now begin to see the originality of Christianity in what it brings with it, what it demands, and in what in itself it alone promises.

The Example of the God-Man

Any attempt to represent Christ as but the consummation of the dynamic processes of Judaism leads to a fundamental misunderstanding of his person. He is first God's Word to Israel and to the world, God's final word, to which nothing may be added, for he is "the very stamp of his nature" (Heb 1:3ff.). As God's Word, he is God, acting for the world; he is God's final and incomparable involvement. For Jesus Christ, being the Son from the first, who of his free love for our sakes fulfills in his own person that obedience owed by man to the God who leads him, on becoming even "under the law" (Gal 4:4), taking its curse upon himself and suffering the condemnation of death that is the law's inseparable companion, through all this openly "disarmed the principalities and powers" (Col 2:15), and defeated the inevitable processes of Jewish dialectic at their source.

By surrendering himself of his own free will in obedience to the Father, the Son has transposed the whole Lord/servant relationship into a new key. The sting of latent rebellion has been withdrawn, and its poison drained. Superfluous now is that revolution of which Judaism dreamed, because its end has already been achieved through man's attaining an inner disposition that makes him love what he is commanded. Between Jesus and his Father there exists no longer any kind of heteronomy (disparity of outlook), but instead, in the communion of the same Holy Spirit, there reigns what can only be described as a homonomy, or parity of outlook; and this is responsible for a fundamental and sudden change in both the form and content of the Old Testament law. For just as the Son's obedience (destined to be put to the most severe test) is the expression of the love he freely gives, so therefore the law appears to him as but the expression of the Father's loving will and is therefore seen by the Son as prescribing what he most of all prefers to do. By this inner disposition, he changes the whole "compulsory nature" of the law; he absorbs its content into himself and transforms it into living language, by means of which the Father whom he loves makes himself understood to him in human terms. For as we saw in Part 1, this was the original way in which the law was meant to be understood.

There are understandably many ways of looking at the change from the Old Testament to the New and there is correspondingly a variety in the language and thought forms in which views of this change can be expressed. It is possible, for example, to look at the much misused Old Testament statically and speak of a break or a new beginning, of "the Law" as opposed to "the Gospel". One can equally distinguish between which parts of the old law were given directly by God, or which came indirectly by Moses' mediation, and what men have added from their traditions, thus falsifying it and laying the emphasis on works (see Mk 7). One can even speak quite simply of a righteousness that far exceeds that of the Old Covenant (see Mt 5:20), and thus is more than sufficient as a fulfillment of the law. In the light of Jesus' obedient sonship, one can describe the new freedom of the Christian as "the principle of faith" (Rom 3:27), the "law of Christ" (Gal 6:2), "the law of the Spirit of life in Christ Jesus" (Rom 8:2), and the Christian correspondingly as the ἔννομος Χριστοῦ, that is, one who is vowed to fulfill the law of Christ. St. James, in particular, underlines the importance of the fact that faith in God's involvement in Christ binds the Christian to a very active involvement in works, and he appeals to the incident of the sacrifice of Isaac as being the type of this.

All these aspects, however, converge to give us a single clear picture. They show us that there can be no question of removing the legal *structures* of existence (as Marx, Freud, Marcuse, and others try to do in order that from there may result a free human disposition) but rather that first of all there must be a change of disposition, which by itself alters the whole status and character of the structures (which in fact cannot be removed). We must go further, however (and here we touch on the eschatological paradox of Christ and the Christians who follow him). In that Jesus, in his loving obedience, accepts from the very outset that death toward which his Father has intended that his life should lead ("for this purpose I have come to this hour"—Jn 12:27), by intentionally accepting this particular death (in which he will find himself abandoned by God), he has already transcended this same death and every other death besides. In this disposition resides already and objectively the resurrection from the dead. Hence all his work for the world this side of death is by him filled with a hope and a "faith" (Heb 12:2) that stretch out way beyond the boundaries of death but in the last resort are founded not on his own power to change the world but rooted in the charge given to him by God, who in "the immeasurable greatness of his power" and "according to the working of his great might" (Eph 1:19), is able to raise the world from the "groaning with labor pains" of wasted efforts and resurrect it from its fallenness (see Rom 8:19ff.).

Let us now look back at that paradox of man, standing in need of "another" (God, the absolute), in order that he may find fulfillment and become his true self. Man's capacity to transcend the structures of this world to which by his very nature he is bound and in which he remains can indeed be the point where God's free involvement makes contact, but is never to be regarded as an assurance that man will eventually attain perfection. In virtue of this capacity for transcendence, man can at least acquire some consciousness of his being captive to the structures, though he would be deceiving himself, should he believe himself capable of freeing himself from this captivity by his own efforts. Nor will he ever attain his full stature as an individual by escaping and immersing himself in mystical or drug-induced experiences, but only by receiving into his merely mortal existence on this earth (of which his capacity for transcendence, his consciousness of "existence unto death" forms a part), by that same divine attitude of mind that Jesus had, and with which Jesus, as God's action has permeated his whole existence. For God, in Christ, there can be no question of avoiding the barriers that men erect or the inevitabilities of human existence. Rather God enters right into the heart of human needs and the narrowness of our existence. "The LORD my God lightens my darkness. Yes, by you I can crush a troop; and by my God I can leap over a wall" (Ps 18:28–29). For man can only finally attain salvation in and through his corporeal existence, his involvement in nature, and his solidarity with the cosmos, and by pursuing the task that was originally given to him to fulfill in this world. Were he to be plucked like a flower or a fruit from the tree of the world and simply transplanted into God, then there would be no justification for the creation itself, nor would there be any cause for man's labors in this world to be taken seriously. Nor could the freedom that God brings by his divine involvement also constitute the fulfillment of man's being that he has been destined to achieve by performing the task delivered to him at his creation. He would be allotted a completely different and again heteronomous kind of freedom that he could never recognize as being the fulfillment of his own innate freedom. It is true, of course, that human freedom can only be fulfilled in God, but it must be a genuinely human freedom that is fulfilled in God. And it can only be this if it treads the difficult path of freedom's trial through the finite conditions of this earthly life; and freedom will only not yield to this test if it is able to possess that hope beyond all hope that God in Jesus Christ accompanies him every step on this way of apparent hopelessness, indwelling and fulfilling its empty capacity for transcendence.

This is the extent to which we must go in order to escape the constant questings of pre-Christian Jewish dialectic. The man who does not finally resolve to follow Christ will in one way or another always fall back into the trammels of this dialectic; for this, and not some remote kind of paganism, is most closely related to his concerns and in a sense a kind of preparatory stage that helped to make Christianity possible, but (as Hegel saw so clearly) which had to be transcended if the true meaning of God's eschatological involvement for us were to come to light.

All this now provides us with the guiding principles for Christian involvement in the world, clear outlines that make us recognize all the difficulties inherent in the apostolic and messianic movement of Christians. The structures of this world are and will always be the structures of the "old Aeon". We must ask now whether it is possible for the spirit of the "new Aeon" in which Christians live in harmony with its hidden reality, to permeate and fill these structures? To what extent can it do this and in what way?

5

THE CHRISTIAN AND THE WORLD

Things and Their Value

The Christian acts within the context of the divine involvement for the freedom of the world. He knows himself to be chosen of God, called by name in fact to assist in this great work of liberation. In this work, man is central, not the angels nor the things of the subhuman creation, brought into being for the sake of man for him to rule over as he was given command by the God who chose him so to do. The Christian must, first of all, learn to see his fellow men and all created things through the eyes of God. This does not mean that man himself, seen in this light, ceases to be a profound mystery. Rather if it is true that God has made him in his own image and likeness, then this ought rather to mean that something of the uniqueness and unfathomableness of God shines in him, so much the clearer to the beholder when God, in choosing him and acting in and for him, sheds upon him his own mysterious light. Man in general—and each individual man in particular—is a mystery. He emerges from the depths of nature (as we have already shown) but, at the same time, transcends nature. On the one hand, he looks to nature, which it is his task to render serviceable and to bring into order; on the other

82

hand, he looks to God, whom he must seek after "in order to find him"—but his capacity for transcendence in itself is no guarantee that he will attain the end for which he was created. This must come to him in freedom. In himself, he constitutes the boundary that divides the world from God (as the Greeks have already remarked), and it is for him to order the things in this world with a view to his own transcendence. He must therefore relate the world to that which lies beyond him, knowing of himself the goal toward which he ought to set his face. The shadows of contradiction lengthen as guilt and death steal over him. He is unable to shut himself up in his own finitude nor enclose himself in his own mortality (for these are realities of his life), leaving the future in the hands of an anonymous ongoing human race and a Providence that has no name, nor can he behave as if his death counted for nothing, and therefore simply busy himself with the usual interests men pursue, preoccupied as they are with the technical administration of the world of things, in which death seems to be of no ultimate significance. The mystery of his being never ceases to nag at him in every possible way.

God alone, acting for man in Christ, takes him completely seriously; and his concern is not just for the species as a whole, but for its every individual representative. For God everything depends on the infinite worth of the person he has chosen, who is called, not just as a private individual for his own sake, but always for the sake of others, for those brothers of his who have not as yet been chosen. "Go therefore and make disciples of all nations" (Mt 28:19); "[G]o to my brethren and say to them, I am ascending to my Father and your Father" (Jn 20:17); "Go home to your friends, and tell them how much the Lord has done for you, and how he has had mercy on you" (Mk 5:19). To be chosen is to be personalized; at the same time it means the drawing of the person out of himself and orientating him toward others, as Paul explains at the end of his great exposition of the theology of history when dealing with the relationship of the Jewish people to the Gentile world (see Rom 9–11). Only God, acting in Christ, takes man's finitude, guilt, and death seriously into account. He does not stand aloof in contempt for the things of this world and the activities to which it is tragically committed, in order to resettle man in a spiritual world on the other side; he relates the whole fiasco of life in this world to the beyond, so that it makes sense, making all man's troubles in the world the foundation for his work of resurrection, salvaging the "mark of the nails" [Jn 20:25] in the glory of eternal life. The sweat and blood of man were not in vain; God acting freely salvages everything when the world is cast in its final and perfect form. Hence in the solution that God offers to this mystery which is man, the tensions still exist, and no aspect of man's being is merely suppressed. For God is great enough to embrace this eternally open being in the even greater expanse of his own openness.

To look through God's eyes at man and at the world means enduring both the openness of man and his contradictions, nor must we try to force them on to a Procrustean bed of dogmatism, but bring all within the sphere of the unity of God's great plan. That man is right whose eyes behold more that is true than other men. This means first that man exists fundamentally as a person, central in God's purposes for he is beloved of God, for him God dies that he may rescue him and draw him to himself. Hence all that has the status of a thing, all that is not personal in this world has value only insofar as it serves the purposes of the person, and is harmful when it betrays the person into the hands of the impersonal, reducing him to slavery and to the status of a thing. This will determine the Christian's attitude toward technology. Man's battle with the universe will always remain something of a struggle and may develop into a violent war, but such a war will be just and permissible only so long as its final aim is always to render man truly human. Only the Christian, however, knows by this struggle who that man is who is to be rendered human, for only the Christian knows about God's love for us, his dying for us, and his Resurrection as the "first fruits of them that are asleep" [1 Cor 15:20]. This man beloved of God is not the man who lives for riches, power, sensual pleasure, and/or his reputation's sake, for the latter misunderstands both himself and all the work he does to organize the world.

We now begin to surmise how difficult it is for the Christian, possessing as he does by the light of the gospel that all-embracing vision of reality, to collaborate with others in the building up of society, when most of those who share this work with him in no way share his vision and even reject it out of hand.

The Opposition of Structures

In an ideal world, the structures of the subhuman creation and those which determine the way society is organized would be so deeply imbued with the spirit of Christianity, that they would completely become instruments for the expression of the love of one person to another and serve toward the establishment of a Christian communion. It is quite clear, however, that should the world be so completely filled with the spirit, then matter would have been transfigured, and this world would be the world after its final resurrection. For in the reality of world history—in the dimension of past, present, and future—the complete salvation of the world has only been accomplished *in spe* (see Rom 8:24; 2 Cor 5:7). And to think that the Christian, by his efforts, is able so radically to change the structures is mere chiliastic fantasy or the hope of an unrealistic enthusiast. The structures belong inseparably to our mortal existence, an existence that is constantly threatened because of guilt and has indeed fallen prey to sin's temptations. The desire to do away altogether with the present order of society and its entirely necessary means of organization leads ultimately to anarchy and takes us not a step further toward the heavenly Jerusalem. Theology as such has no obvious direct competence to make pronouncements on the structure of the secular world and simply sends the Christian into the world with an image of man, whereby and according to which he is to organize its structures as responsibly and intelligently as he can. He must not overlook the fact, however, that the world's structures belong to the realm of finitude and "futility" (Rom 8:20); he should not forget that they are merely contingent and, casting all political judgment to the winds, demand, for example, total disarmament or a policy of nonresistance or pacifism from motives of Christian charity and Christian principles of communion. Such ideals are indeed justifiable objectives, but to want to put them into practice suddenly would seem to indicate a grave lack of a sense of responsibility.

This again does not mean that the Christian must simply resign himself to the world as it is now and ever shall be. The Christian's task is so far as he is able to fill the structures of the world with the boundless spirit of love and reconciliation, despite the fact that he will always encounter opposition to his efforts toward this end. There will of necessity always be compromises. To take a common example: a Christian architect is given the task of designing a modern hospital. His general plan will look quite different from those of an atheist because he has taken into consideration the importance of the sick as people. Central to his conception is this concern for the person rather than the smooth-running apparatus in which the patient as an individual becomes submerged. He will find it possible to pursue this emphasis just so far, but then technical considerations come into play and it is suggested that a fully "humanized" hospital is basically impracticable. Again some director of public prosecutions will, in the course of dealing with the accused, attempt to exhibit a high degree of Christian humanitarian feeling, but yet feel compelled to protect the interests of the state and society in his case. It would be remarkably fortunate if he were able to convince the accused, when sentenced, that the punishment meted out to him was in fact awarded in his own and better interests.

What we have just said about the effectiveness of the individual Christian in the world holds good also for communities of Christians who would like to set an example to the world by the Christian spirit of their life together. Apart from the fact that the members of such communities have this advantage, that they are able to strengthen one another in Christian living and, by this mutual exchange within their society, make life in the spirit of Christianity more credible to the world, they are nevertheless still bound up with the secular structures of society and feel their impact whether inside the community or in their relations with the non-Christian world around them. In encountering these secular structures, they come up against the kind of opposition one might expect. Like mortal man, all structures of life in

this world suffer from an ambivalence that it is impossible
to resolve. Man in his freedom is always capable of mis-
using them; they can be the instruments of his lust for power,
in fact, for the creation of any kind of disorder. The attempt
to establish such a model of a Christian community within
the wider community of man will be a kind of challenging
signal, which shows man the way he should go, the values
he should respect, and how to give life to the structures of
this world from within. The challenging signal will attract
the more attention in proportion as it refuses to close its
doors against the world and as it refuses to make the claim
to have discovered all and therefore to be infallible. Rather,
it should stand open to all who are compelled to live among
those same structures that characterize the life of all men. If
it does this then it will not appear as some icon from another
world, but, rather, as a shining witness to God's actions for
the sake of this world.

With this Christian group as our example, we ought now
to make a foray into the whole question of the Church and
its structures; this really would be going beyond our brief
and we shall only touch on this matter. For the question is
a great deal more complex than that of the group, because
the structures of the visible Church are at their deepest roots
devised by the love of God. (Therefore they cannot be a
suitable subject for investigation by the sociologists of religion.) They are crystallizations, so to speak, of the divine
love, which love itself has bestowed upon the Church, in
order that she may not have to depend on the contingency
of personal relationships that do not last. Of this nature are
structures such as the sacraments, holy Scripture, and also,
of course, the ordained ministry. But as these crystallizations of the divine love are manifested in the sphere of the
temporal and used by sinful men who also place their own

interpretation on their meaning, so these structures also fall within the sphere of man's capacity to misuse them and to change their meaning. They therefore need to feel the breath of the authentic spirit of Christian love blowing through them in order to be credible. Throughout the centuries, Christians—priests as well as laymen—fall prey to the temptation to endow isolated structures, authorities, and institutions with the quality of the sacred, and in doing this they inevitably call forth protests from the Church and invite revolution and open confrontation. It is nonetheless still possible to maintain that the structures of the Church are more easily permeated than those of the world, however convinced one may be, on sociological grounds, that the contrary is true (for example, with regard to the priesthood today). The structures of the Church already contain something of the quality of the New Age, and one cannot say that they will not attain fulfillment in the risen life to come. For all eternity, the New Jerusalem, as portrayed in the Book of Revelation, is built on "twelve foundations" on which "the twelve names of the twelve apostles of the Lamb" are inscribed (Rev 21:14). The Church's primary task therefore is, by constantly subjecting herself to self-criticism in the light of the judgment of Christ, to make her structures as far as possible transparent to Christian love, so that the Church as a whole may witness purely to God's action in the world. This she will never fully succeed in doing; the sinfulness of man prevents the framework of the Church's structure being filled with love to its very limits, though it was to be filled with love that this framework first was fashioned. The Christian's work, however, of making the Church's structures transparent to what they really contain is carried out in their work as Christians of the Church in the service of the world.

Work and Witness

The Christian, being a man who lives in fellowship with others, is of course committed to taking part in mankind's common effort toward the humanizing of the world, the problematic and indeed tragic nature of which we have already earlier indicated. The Christian, however, has no clear-cut recipe or solution to offer to this problem and like others has to wrestle with the deciphering of the riddles of nature and of history. In this pursuit he is at one with all his fellow men; but knowing as he does how God acts in the world, his horizons are made wider by this, for his greater vision embraces all the problems and the tragedies of the world without removing them, and from his vision comes the only light that can illuminate the darkness of the world and come to its assistance. It is for him to be a witness to this light, not merely by an abstract confession of his faith, but concretely in all the work he does in his vocation and with his fellow men. Under certain circumstances this witness can take the form of a protest, and does so when the world, surrounding him with its plans and demanding his compliance, declares openly its intention to go against God's involvement for the sake of the world.

Yet this dilemma has always faced the Christian, from the time when the first Christian apologists made their declaration of loyalty to the Roman emperor; their appeals, however, resounded with the proviso that a greater obedience was owed to God the Father of their Lord Jesus Christ (cf. Acts 5:29), to the time when Russian Christians vowed loyalty to the Soviet regime—recognizing here achievements in the social sphere that "Christianity had not brought about by its own efforts"—yet at the same time refusing to engage in dialogue about the difference between the

fundamental positions of theism and atheism (cf. the lec-
tures of Nikodim [Rotov] given to the World Council of
Churches at Uppsala). There is nothing, and indeed no one,
who can liberate the Christian from this dilemma in which
he has been placed and must remain, on account of the
pact he has made with God and his action for the world.
The Christian himself is not responsible for the dilemma; it
is the ambiguity of the world that makes it so, for the world
hovers between behaving like a good creation and shutting
itself up in an attitude of hostility to the love of God; such
ambiguity will never be removed while this age lasts, for it
is a constituent factor in its composition.

This being so, the Christian must now ask what kind of
a position he ought to adopt to make his actions appear
completely unambiguous in the constantly changing cli-
mate of this world's values. When can he cooperate? When,
for example, must he refuse to cooperate and change to a
policy of resistance in order that he may make his act of
witness? Should this question of how to behave in a situation that is constantly changing its colors never permit of
his answering it unambiguously? Is he then not likely to
remain uncertain whenever he is asked to commit himself
and even begin to change his own position? But the consequence of this surely is that the various parties within the
Church become more and more estranged from one another.
On the one hand, there are the progressives with their plans
for cooperating as fully as possible with the world; on the
other hand, there are the *intégristes* or conservatives, who
openly display the Church's exclusive plan, impressive in its
monolithicity. But to divide these two necessary tendencies
into two such radically opposed camps means that we give
up all hope of mastering the concrete situation. The first of
these positions is right, insofar as the Christian is not required

to offer the world its own set programs of action, but is, rather, called to involve himself in working for and in the world with God in Jesus Christ. There is right, too, in the other position insofar as the Christian's action must always be rooted in the source, which is God's action, and must itself be vindicated by reference to the source. To move away progressively from the source out into the world is an action specifically condemned in the New Testament ("[a]ny one who goes ahead and does not abide in the doctrine of Christ does not have God"—2 Jn 9); but to remain at the Alpha, which, if we did, would bind us to the past and not release us to stride out toward the freedom of the Omega, would mean our failing to cooperate with God's working in the world, and this would be directly contrary to the whole idea of the Christian's essentially missionary existence, which is the peculiar form of Christian existence (see Jn 17:18; 20:21). Our way must somehow lie between the two.

Here, we should do well to remember before everything else God's promised gift of the Holy Spirit, who will not only help Christians toward a profounder understanding of what the Lord has said to them or merely hinted at (see Jn 16:13ff.) but will also give them the appropriate words to say in moments of difficulty and danger (see Mt 10:18ff.). Certainly, whoever would wish to possess the Spirit to inspire him in a given situation must abide in the source where the Spirit blows, that is, between the Father and the Son; he must therefore continue in prayer and in self-denial, and in readiness for any task he may be sent to do. But in the Spirit he will be enabled both to see and to follow the straight course of action he must pursue, which means that by his behavior as a Christian he will be able to bring to bear a measure of unambiguity on ambiguous situations, and by his decisiveness will move others toward a right decision when they are unable to see the same situation in so clear a light. The Spirit therefore operates through the Christian, making all clear even in the non-Christian world. This does not release the Christian from the obligation of studying carefully the complexities of a situation, and of accepting it as such. On no account must he behave like one of those frightful simplifiers; for it is not for him, as we have already said, to attempt to cleave the complexities of the domain of the secular with the sword-edge of some theological argument. The Holy Spirit does not work through him in this way. Rather, it is one of his characteristics that he takes the things of this earth and by moving them from within makes them clear (see Rom 8:26ff.).

In this process of clarification, however, a boundary also becomes apparent, that limit to which a Christian can still responsibly go and which marks the stage at which he must say No. This No, which classes the Christian as a confessor and if necessary as a martyr, is nothing less than an authentic continuation of the original Yes, accepting God's eschatological action for the world. If we look at it objectively, martyrdom is nothing less than pure triumphant joy that "the Son of God, Jesus Christ, whom we preached among you, Silvanus and Timothy and I, was not Yes and No; but in him it is always Yes. For all the promises of God find their Yes in him. That is why we utter the Amen through him, to the glory of God" (2 Cor 1:19–20). When the Christian confesses his faith in God's Yes, this is a sign that God has finally committed himself to the world, therefore in itself this confession is not unrelated to the world, it is not the confession of a religious fanatic, but it is simply the logical conclusion of the single-mindedness of the commitment made by the Christian as a responsible fellow man for the whole world.

6

THE JOY OF THE CROSS

"Falling into the Earth"

Most of the criticisms made against the Church are directed against what used, until recently, to be called "the hierarchy", but what we now call, more simply, the ministry. In view of the fact that the ministers of the Church have been given special responsibility to guide the faithful and to this end have been appointed as "apostles, prophets, evangelists, pastors, and teachers" (see Eph 4:11) to "equip the saints for the work of ministry, for building up the body of Christ" (see Eph 4:12), they ought therefore to resign themselves to the fact that when the buck is passed, it finally stops with them. To give it its proper degree of importance in the Church, the ministry is in fact by no means a kind of "foreign ministry" for the Church; we could rather compare it perhaps to the skeleton that enables a living organism to walk upright, and though rigid itself, gives flexibility to the rest and is wholly concealed within the living body. It is, of course, possible that the ministry will in time to come once more play a concealed and therefore more effective part in the life of the Church, thus enabling the Church of the faithful, those lively little congregations which have always constituted the "outer skin" of the Church, where the

94

Church brushes against the world around her, to reassume their place in the front rank, one could even say, to be pushed into the front line of fire. For the Church's credibility will in the future depend on those who represent her in the world.

It is becoming increasingly difficult to identify these representatives of the Church, because there is such a variety of them and they are so scattered and divided. It is impossible to classify them under one heading or to find a common denominator that suits them all. Only the faith that they confess in common, which demands that they themselves should be its living witness, can be the title to include them all. If this is so, then the Church will no longer be judged by her credal formulas, still less by the utterances of her theologians, but by the inner meaning of her creeds that lies behind their formulas and phrases, by what they promise of the grace of God, and by the demands they make on men in all their actions. Those theologians and other Christians who play about with these creeds in order to present them in a more modern and acceptable form will as a matter of course no longer hold the limelight. We are slowly returning to the realization that those of the faithful who stand out by the way in which they live the Church's faith, who used to be called "saints" (whether they were canonized or not), are the people in whose hands lies the whole destiny of the Church of today and tomorrow and who will determine whether or not the Church will achieve recognition in the world. It is by no means necessary that such "saints" as these should be exceptional individuals. Some have such a calling, but they are few and far between. And these are often only the spark that kindles a group, be it great or small, which does the work of spreading the new light that shone in its founder in the scattered places of the world. The members of such groups may devote themselves especially to prayer and devoted service for the world within the context of a religious order, in which case their light will automatically be almost hidden from the eyes of men. They may, alternatively, make their way into the non-Christian world, having formed themselves into loosely knit groups or associations, thus living "close to the earth" (which is what humility actually means) and will therefore always be prepared to sink like "a grain of mustard seed" or "grain of wheat", wherever the earth should open up to let them in. This often happens so unobtrusively that afterward people are amazed when "the full harvest" comes or "the greatest of all trees in the garden" grows, for they are unable to trace either of these back to their origins. But it is only because something authentically Christian has appeared that one can confidently say, looking back, that something authentically Christian must have been sunk into the earth. And such authentic Christianity will give the world a great deal more to worry about than the towering edifices of the hierarchy.

When the triumphalism of the hierarchy has been brought low, however, there still remains a more subtle spiritual kind of triumphalism, the triumphalism one finds expressed in the ideologies of groups or small parishes. This has been the source—from the days of Paul, John, and the Gnostics—of those sects professing to be the "true unspotted Church". And these are made up of people who as individuals or as communities arrogate to themselves the Church's quality of holiness. That small groups should exhibit the virtue of humility is perhaps more than anything else necessary for the Church today, but at the same time this virtue is instinct with danger since, on the one hand, they may be tempted to become too involved with the world and, on the other hand, tempted to become enclosed and too autonomous. The only solution to this lies in their being open to receive God's revelation in its fullest catholicity, to receive the fullness of God's saving work in Christ that is impatient of any hasty or summary explanation, cannot be limited to the dimensions of human certainty, nor copied and reproduced by our attempts at Christian living nor in our programs and designs for our activities, but always towers above us as the infinitely and eternally greater. It is the Holy Spirit himself who gives the person ready to receive him an instinctive apprehension of this catholicity, an instinct as sharp in the old woman praying her Rosary as in the academic who methodically plans his course of action or in the theologian who is looking for the most meaningful way of talking about God's action in the world.

We plead, therefore, for "a poor and servant Church", because only such a Church can be sure of making contact with the world of today, not because she desires to be successful, but because she feels it is her duty so to do. We are looking, in fact, for a Church that so long as she is able to be effective in the world, cooperates with the world in its endeavors, yet which knows for certain from her knowledge of her Master's fate that where men's actions cease to be outwardly effective and where suffering, sickness, and evident failure make their entry, there her work does not cease, but rather begins in earnest. Such a Church has torn down her ramparts that protect her from the world; she sees herself no longer as a "stronghold sure" but rather as a model for God's greater purposes; for God's concern is with the world, and the Church is but the mediator of his purposes. Perhaps God allows as much of the Church to survive as he needs for leaven to mix with the dough, or for new corn whose only purpose is to fall into the earth and die that it may be raised as something else. This affords us a totally new and dynamic understanding of tradition; we can no longer see it as simply the handing on of what always was. For in a living tradition, at every moment the original *traditio* (that is, the surrender of the Son by the Father for the salvation of the world) is repeated. And in the process of eternally surrendering herself in imitation of God's act of self-surrender (as we see exemplified by St. Paul when he lays down his apostolic labors—see Acts 20:17–38; Phil 2:17ff.; 2 Tim) the Church lives in a perpetual process of death and resurrection within the living source of the tradition.

A Sign of Joy in the Universal Darkness

How does this happen? If this grain of wheat, the Christian, really and truly falls into the darkness of the earth, if he disintegrates and becomes entirely mixed with earth, will he not then become involved in the whole uncertainty of human destiny, such as is experienced by his non-Christian brethren? Will he not feel for and with them, thankful perhaps for being granted such an experience?—for it is this that underlies the establishment of any true community. Will he not realize that the conscious dogmatism of Christian teaching is but a final wall of separation, a last fling of triumphalism that one would readily abandon? Did not Paul, too, become all things to all men (1 Cor 9:22), and did he not command all Christians to rejoice with those who rejoice and to weep with those who weep (Rom 12:15)? There is, however, a quite clear limit to these actions of an apostle. Paul would have never recommended the Christian to be unbelieving with the unbelievers, nor even to doubt with those who doubt. For Christian faith is the pivot of all he says and does.

There is an objection, however, even to this. Did not Christ on the Cross venture so deeply into the darkness enveloping all the sinful? Did he not become so solidly at one with them to the extent of desiring to share with them their state of being abandoned by God? We can only reply to this in easy stages. First, the abandonment of Christ is God's way of acting for us all. Christ abandoned fulfills uniquely, alone and by himself, all that God had promised; on the Cross it is quite clearly he whom all have forsaken and abandoned; he is betrayed by Christians, denied by the Jews as their Messiah, thrust aside by the pagan world as being unwanted, and finally executed at their hand. But only after this lonely suffering of the One for the sake of all did men (after the Resurrection and in the power of the Resurrection) in a way begin to follow Christ. As we saw earlier, the Christian, by faith and baptism, has been immersed in the whole Christ event; he lives and dies with Christ and with him is raised again. And these three constitute a single indivisible whole and together form the good news that God has acted for our liberation.

Here we can go on to our second point. If we are called to follow God in his action in Christ, for us to live and to be called to live in the whole movement of God's saving work is in itself pure joy; it is the grace of Easter. This is the Church's joy; it is objective, not primarily individual or psychological, but it is impossible that we should feel nothing of the joy of God and of his Church, rooted as it is in God's great saving work for us, when we both receive and give our assent to the true faith. This joy is Christian joy and pervades all things. "With all our affliction, I am overjoyed" (2 Cor 7:4). "Count it all joy, my brethren, when you meet various trials" (Jas 1:2). And the Christian ought to be humble enough to accept this gift of joy that God bestows on him as one of "God's poor", nor should he resist this gift as poor men are renowned for doing in their pride. He ought to receive it as grace from God. For himself alone, however? Surely he receives it just as much, perhaps even more so in order that he may share it and hand it on to others. It is perhaps just this Christian joy in all its many forms that those around me most direly need from me. But what joy can they have from me if I am just another doubter in their midst? What else are they looking for in me, if it is not a spark of faith in love and light?

Only now can we mention our third point. God distributes his gifts as he will. From the treasury of Christian grace, he can select individual pieces that he earmarks for this or that person in particular. As the Curé of Torcy explains to his young friend in Bernanos' novel *The Diary of a Country Priest*, in Christ's following we all have our special place. Our place can be on the Mount of Olives or at any one of the Stations of the Cross. In such a place, however, it is possible that the Christian, in some special way that somehow is suited to his calling, will be led again and again into situations where he finds himself abandoned by God. God can bring about such situations as he will; they differ in intensity as in the length of time they last and the frequency with which they recur. They may be situations that could be described as mystical (in the narrower sense of that term), like the dark night of St. John of the Cross. On the other hand, they may be brought about by external events, as, for example, by the cruelty of concentration camps or the gas chambers, or by the torture chambers of so many a modern totalitarian state. On this subject of the fearsomeness of God's grace we can add two comments. First, that no Christians may seek it or acquire it by themselves, nor even should they be seeking to share the lot of their fellow men. The most a Christian could do would be to be allowed to ask God that if it should so please him, he might vicariously experience some of the darkness of his fellow men. But God alone can decide this. It is also true to say that such grace will only be given between two joys, in any case it will only be given within the context of an all-embracing experience of Christian joy, even if the latter is only restored when man passes from this life to God (which is not envisaged in the classical teaching of St. John of the Cross). Within the fiery darkness of suffering, into which the individual Christian may be plunged, there gleams a light, a ray from that first Light, of which the suffering is a consequence, as Jesus' abandonment on Calvary is the consequence and the expression of his perfect love.

Most Christians will experience periods of darkness in the life of faith, which are a long way from being as intense as the dark nights of the great mystics. But the darknesses of the normal life of faith are, however, felt more intensively today in the general atmosphere of uncertainty, and we tend to be more conscious of them when they come our way. Christians who experience this should remember that the life of faith must hover freely between the Alpha and the Omega; it is an existence that does not permit of our faith being able to turn back on itself, in order to be reassured rationally about itself, as we humans might like to do. For in that faith is more than any establishable synthesis of reason (seen as knowledge), in that it is an act of the whole living human being and not merely the exercising of one of his functions (that is, the function of reason), it is therefore basically both impossible and indeed contradictory that faith's content (which is God freely revealing himself) should be "proved" or that faith as an act (man responding freely to God) should be elicited from man as some logically necessary response. The whole free swing that marks the act of faith can just as well fill man with a joyful sense of liberation as it can fill him with a sense of panic-stricken anxiety through being suddenly exposed. Both are understandable, both are adventitious. The decisive factor in the act of faith is the taking of the risk of surrendering ourselves to the freedom and love of God.

The best thing a Christian can do, therefore, is in no way to wish to be the master of his own moods, but simply to allow himself to be led by his living faith into whatever is presented to him in the course of time. Again to be led by faith means to remain in perpetual contact with the source and to have no desire to seek one's own adventure. The greatest adventure after all is God's redeeming action for the world in his Son, and if we follow the Son's course we shall not run the risk of losing ourselves on the slippery paths of self-inverted love. "In this is love, not that we loved God but that he loved us and sent his Son to be the expiation for our sins" (1 Jn 4:10).

Little Flock and Great World

When we talked earlier about the Church of today, saying that she is becoming more humble and more closely related to the world, and that what up to now had appeared as her outer structures are becoming a feature of her interior life, we thereby intimated that wherever the Church is seen to be truly the Church, she is inevitably but a small flock of faithful people. Her life radiates from small centers, scattered all over the world, like the lights of homesteads when darkness falls over the countryside. It is at these centers that man enters into the experience of the love of God in Christ, both sacramentally and existentially, in the life of prayer and through the experience of the mutual exchange of love; and the kind of life experienced by this small community can thence be carried out by its members as individuals and by the community as a whole into the world of non-Christians. But in the process of communicating his life in the small group to the world, the Christian may have the new and rather confusing experience of discovering that most of what he brings with him to the world has in some way or another already reached the world, not in its entirety, of course, but only in fragments; it is not recognized for what it is but only acknowledged subconsciously or simply taken for granted, nor is it by any means gladly accepted, but, rather, in advance, the world turns its back on it and rejects at least the caricatures by which Christianity is so frequently represented. For the images of God and of the Church of Christ that circulate in the world are so incredibly grotesque, that one can scarcely be surprised that there are so many vowed to atheism, so many hostile to the Church.

Jesus himself, of course, on several occasions experienced this phenomenon of Christianity already having arrived in the world before he did. When he met the Syrophoenician woman for example (see Mk 7:24ff.), or the Roman centurion (see Mt 8:5ff.), he said on each occasion, "I have not found so great faith, no not in Israel." Only the foreigner, the Samaritan, thanks him for having healed him (see Lk 17:16); it is another Samaritan who becomes the model of a Christian's love for his neighbor (see Lk 10:25ff.); and a woman from Samaria becomes the occasion of his first genuine wave of conversions (see Jn 4:39ff.). On the larger scale it is the Gentiles who are not closely associated with him, rather than the Jews who are closely related to him, who accept the gospel message, and this is often foretold in the sayings of Jesus and confirmed by the narrative of the Acts of the Apostles. It is almost as if the longing and the hunger of people who have to go without is a better preparation for the completely unexpected than the hopes of those who have already formed for themselves on the basis of the promises a firm picture of that which is to come. For the picture they form blocks the way for God when he eventually comes, whereas the pagans, having no preconceived notions, are able to receive him.

And then, throughout the centuries of the Church's history, there is a diffused spread—I don't say of the grace of God among all people, for it is impossible to form an overall picture of how this happens and we have no empirical data by which to form such a picture—but of Christian teaching, which in innumerable ways, both open and concealed, has made its way into the world and has infiltrated some worldviews quite foreign to itself. One has only to think of how much biblical material has been propagated through the Koran, and also how the Indian code of ethics has been transformed through its contact with Christianity, despite the fact that its formulators were scarcely conscious of Christianity at all. This is to leave unmentioned all the innumerable sects and denominations that exist like so many distant suburbs of a central conurbation, yet who knows how much of the spirit from the center these sects have carried with them to the boundaries. In contemplating this phenomenon, we can see in a new way how God's grain of corn falls into the earth and dies and, in a way we cannot clearly discern, rises again and continues its life under a new and strange form. From God's point of view, this strange growth from his seed is often more vigorous than another growth that calls itself Christian but deliberately turns away from the center and strides out on its own.

All this, however, can give new heart to the little flock. Not only is God for her (and therefore who can be against her?—see Rom 8:32), but God has also prepared for her many confederates in his work, when she thought that she had been left entirely alone. In the Gospels, Jesus sends his disciples to places where he himself will follow afterward. In the history of the Church, however, he hastens on in front of them, and they often find him already there in some way when they arrive. This, however, should not make them any less concerned to make an effort. They are much needed. We, whom God has made free, are God's partners in bringing to the world its freedom. And Christianity must always, historically speaking, flow out into the world from a living and glowing center—there is already enough dead lava lying around. For liberal Christianity that has shed its dogmas still from time to time succeeds in reflecting from afar something of the core of true religion, but has not the original penetrating power of the Christianity that is rooted in the source at the center. Only that inner circle that centers its life on God's action in the Christ event has this power. For this inner circle is the community of those for whom the Word had not grown cold and become just abstract doctrine, but is the living personal presence of the Trinity, articulated in their life of brotherly love and a communion that is both sacramental and existential. Wherever in the world such a community exists, there is the source whence the world's true liberation begins.

Here, too, man is saved from the fear of being challenged by atheistic schemes for human freedom. For all such schemes, together with Christianity itself, are being challenged by the stark realities of the natural world (whose aggressive character we took pains to stress in the Introduction), and they can only cope with these hard facts of life by proposing some *Utopia* that transcends them. In this world the Lord/servant relationship will never fully be removed (Marx); man will never wholly come to terms with his origins and integrate them into his personality (Freud); he will never in this world be the superman who is indebted to no one for what he has to give generously (Nietzsche); nor will he ever be able in this world to conjure up out of his own person that *homo absconditus* who is truly free (Bloch); nor fashion for himself a nature that knows no principle of aggression (Marcuse). The Christian design for freedom is much broader than any of those schemes because he does not only go out to find freedom, in a life that ends in death (as the Stoics and the Buddhists do), but transcends this kind of freedom by his free faith in Christ whereby he knows that God will bring him, whole and entire, together with all his fellow men, with history and the cosmos to their final salvation "on the third day".